* * * * * * * *

Copyright (c) 2005 by Rich
(exclusive of U.S. War Department documents ;
Chugg)

* * * * * * * *

ISBN 0 9518934 4 0

* * * * * * * *

By the same author

"Spirits of the sand"

History of the U.S. Army WWII Assault Training Center in North Devon, England. From formation of the Center and creation of the American assault doctrine for Normandy, includes training details of the combat troops who would spearhead the American amphibious assault on the beaches of Normandy. The ATC is an area overshadowed by the very event it made possible - D Day June 6th 1944. A story never before told from archive documents, maps and recollections of those who served and trained there.

"Precious cargo"

Wartime history of the U.S. Army 146th QM Truck Company - from peacetime formation as a National Guard outfit traces their chase across North Africa with the British 8th Army. To England and their significant part in the aftermath of the Exercise Tiger disaster. In the front lines of Normandy and Brittany, the race across Europe, running the Red Ball Highway, and rushing reinforcements into the Battle of the Bulge. Crossing the Rhine at Remagen and into Berlin. Told exclusively from veteran's recollections.

"Brigades of Neptune"

A comprehensive history of the WWII U.S. Army Engineer Special Brigades and their component units. From formation and training in England to D-Day itself as told by surviving veterans. For six months the Brigades brought supplies, men vehicles and equipment across the open beaches of Normandy. A story never before told using archive material, personal documents, photographs and statistical data.

"Clear the way"

Unit history of the 146th Engineer Combat Battalion. From formation to England and the Assault Training Center, through the hell of D-Day ahead of the infantry on Omaha beach. Bridge building and fighting their way across Europe into Berlin and eastern Europe. Told from veteran's recollections, documents and photographs.

Websites: www.assaulttrainingcenter.com
www.rtbassbooks.com

ACKNOWLEDGEMENTS

I am grateful to everyone who has contributed to this publication in all manner of ways, whether practical or by permission. All have given whole-hearted support to this project and their enthusiasm has maintained the momentum needed to achieve such outstanding results.

Mr Raymond Coldwell of Christie Estates – the owners of Braunton Burrows – has always given his enthusiastic support and shown a keen interest in the exploration of the Assault Training Centre by allowing practical research to be carried out in such a sensitive area.

The Ministry of Defence (Army) who use Braunton Burrows for military exercises have always given their utmost co-operation in advising availability of certain areas.

Shirley Blaylock of the National Trust – stewards of Baggy Point – allowed me to accompany her archaeological survey of that area which proved of great mutual benefit. Allowing me to visit the Assault Training Centre's constructions on property that is not open to the public, and securing their future preservation.

I am indebted to every single member of "First Wave 44" for their hard work and keenness in literally uncovering many of the sites. With their combined expertise, the identification of artefacts found is both accurate and definitive, and invaluable in appreciating the usage of individual sites.

English Nature has an especial interest in Braunton Burrows and close co-operation with Mr. John Breeds has ensured that their interests have always been preserved.

Of invaluable help and guidance to the project has been Mr. Adrian Wilton. As the MoD warden, his detailed knowledge of Braunton Burrows is unsurpassed and his practical guidance is invaluable.

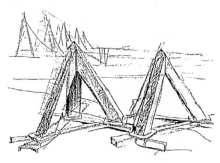

INDEX

FOREWORD

The true significance of the wartime Assault Training Center and its vital contribution to the success of D-Day was only revealed at Woolacombe in May 1992.

Since closure in April 1944 it had lain dormant. For the previous six months this whole area of North Devon had been crowded with American soldiers, speeding army vehicles, lumbering construction machinery, and the almost non-stop distant sound of explosions. The village pubs overflowed with boisterous young men in American uniforms, and the trans-Atlantic twang could be heard in all the shops. Then one day they were all gone. Peace and an eerie silence settled over the towns and villages with a premonition that their disappearance meant a new episode of World War II was about to unfold.

Within weeks it happened. On 6th June 1944 the greatest amphibious assault in military history was launched against the coast of Normandy marking the beginning of the end of Nazi supremacy in Europe. And at the spearhead of these landings were the American friends of North Devon.

D-Day heralded a string of wartime events avidly followed by the eyes and ears of the world through to eventual and inevitable victory for the Allied nations, followed by a long dreamt of peace and return to normality.

Once requisitioned hotels in Woolacombe again hosted traditional family holidaymakers attracted by the golden sands and Atlantic surf of North Devon. Croyde and Saunton once more became sleepy villages, and the whole of North Devon was now enjoying peace and prosperity as its traditional industries of agriculture and tourism flourished.

Saunton golf course reconstructed its fairways and greens, and Baggy Point was being farmed again under the stewardship of the National Trust.

Areas used by the military were returned to their owners and in 1947 a thorough sweep was made of Braunton Burrows for unexploded and abandoned ordnance. Vegetation here flourished almost unchecked and its contours constantly changed at the whim of the elements, smothering wartime constructions.

The American occupation was all but forgotten.

Until May 1992, when a memorial dedicated to all those soldiers who had trained here was unveiled by the wartime commandant of the Assault Training Center, Brigadier General Paul W. Thompson. This event coincided with the publication of "Spirits of the sand", a detailed history of this unique establishment and its vital contribution to the American success on D-Day.

Since then practical research has been carried out to locate, identify and record all American wartime constructions. Those demolished in the late 1940's are lost forever, only their images remaining in faded photographs. But most have been found and explored with the help of computer technology, archive maps and plans, unexpected fresh information from both sides of the Atlantic, and chance discoveries of wartime artefacts.

This "Field Edition" details what has been discovered so far as research continues to locate lost constructions.

OVERVIEW

Boundaries of the U.S. Assault Training Centre reservation were drawn early in 1943 by Lieutenant Colonel Paul W. Thompson. His mission was two-fold. Firstly, to produce doctrine for assaulting a heavily defended enemy coastline. And having done that from scratch, he then had to train combat troops in those principles. As Commandant of the only American establishment tasked with training soldiers for the anticipated invasion of Europe, he soon realised that the very success or failure of the American D-Day landings lay fully upon his shoulders.

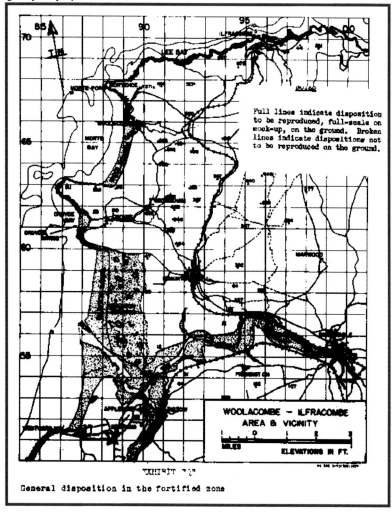

Full lines indicate disposition to be reproduced, full-scale on mock-up, on the ground. Broken lines indicate disposition not to be reproduced on the ground.

WOOLACOMBE – ILFRACOMBE
AREA & VICINITY

ELEVATIONS IN FT.

EXHIBIT "A"

General disposition in the fortified zone

All good training areas had already been claimed by the British so Thompson had no choice but to accept the Atlantic coast around Woolacombe. A coastline the British deemed too rough and stormy for training. The perimeter of the land he required here for full-scale military manoeuvres followed the railway line south from Mortehoe Station to Braunton, and the River Caen to the Taw and Torridge estuary. Every acre to the west of this line he needed for exercises and rehearsals using live ammunition, explosives, tanks, artillery and air support.

But nestling in this region were several picturesque Devon villages - Croyde, Putsborough, Georgeham and Saunton. The task before Thompson at this stage included not only the neutralisation of enemy beach defences, but also the fight inland off the beaches, and these settlements were in his way. They would have to be evacuated along with all the farms and smaller settlements, and Thompson told the American High Command there was no other option.

After weeks of frustrating inactivity it seemed to Thompson that the British were dragging their heels, depriving him of precious time to activate his training base and several of his urgent memoranda prompted no response whatsoever. He was being pressed to establish the Assault Training Center, but without confirmation he could use the land he wanted, he could make no plans.

Unexpectedly he was advised that his mission had been reduced. He no longer had to teach troops to fight their way inland past the enemy beach defences, just get them through the coastal fortifications.

There were several reasons for this dramatic change. The American High Command had found an alternative area where amphibious-landed troops would assume the beach defences had been overcome, and could practice establishment of a bridgehead and moving inland. That area lay just behind Slapton beach in South Devon. A more sinister reason for dividing Thompson's initial two-fold mission was the higher command estimates of casualty rates which they believed would leave the assaulting units fully spent after the assault, and establishment of the bridgehead would have to rely upon rapid reinforcement.

The mission reduction however was a tactical relief for the ATC staff who could now concentrate their efforts to provide training programmes, lessons, exercises and practical problems for the infantry and engineers in their individual and combined tasks to hit the enemy shore and break through the crust of beach defences.

Beaches within the reservation were ideal for basic and advanced amphibious exercises despite the fierce Atlantic surf, and Woolacombe Sands was soon found to be identical to "Omaha" in nearly every respect of sand quality, beach gradient, and tide range. Anyone who has seen Omaha beach will instantly notice an uncanny resemblance to Woolacombe and Saunton.

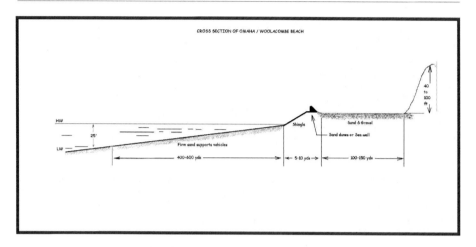

Training troops to successfully overcome enemy beach defences required ranges for all weapons that would be used in the assault to ensure proficiency in handling, accuracy and repeated exercises in tactics of the new doctrine against accurate replicas of what they would encounter on the enemy shore.

Construction of these ranges and training aids - mostly replicas of German pillboxes - had to be done quickly as the training schedule already drawn up had the first units arriving in North Devon on 1st September 1943.

To build them U.S. Army Southern Base Section had assigned the 398th Engineer General Service Regiment who had only just arrived in England ... " On August 7th we located ourselves on a hill a mile west of Braunton, North Devon. In fields bounded by stone walls, we pitched our pup tents for the first time on European soil. At night we learned that English soil was no softer than that found in United States on bivouac problems. With issuance of construction missions, Companies were scattered in all directions. Companies C and E were located one and two miles, respectively, west of Braunton. Company D established itself one mile north of Bideford. Company F set up camp a half mile south of Croyde. And Second Battalion Headquarters operated from Saunton Sands".

With winter looming, a permanent camp was needed to supplement the tented encampments at Lincombe, Woolacombe, Croyde and Braunton. Just outside Braunton the 398th constructed ... " 505 Nissen huts for quarters, dispensaries, showers, ablutions and mess halls to comprise a camp capable of housing 4250 men. We laid 5000 feet of sewer line and 8700 feet of water line. "

The overall reservation boundaries remained as originally drawn but now, after the mission reduction, contained areas not needed by the military, so only those that would see action had boundaries drawn around them and were letter-coded.

The existing road network of narrow country lanes was assessed for movement of troops, trucks and tanks, some being so narrow for military traffic they were designated one-way. For ease of navigation road junctions were numbered, and where no roads existed new temporary tracks were constructed.

The Assault Training Centre had a progressive, fluid policy based on the early receipt of intelligence on German beach defences so they could immediately produce counter tactics. As a consequence of this constant up-dating, layouts of some training aids were altered, some added to, others removed or even abandoned between September 1943 and March 1944.

The majority of training aid sites on Braunton Burrows and Baggy Point are pillbox "faces" - solid concrete blocks of pillbox dimensions with a sculpted or painted embrasure as an aiming point.

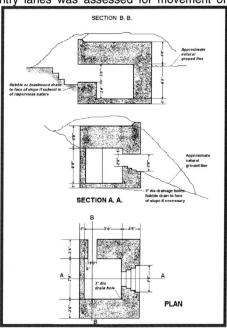

6

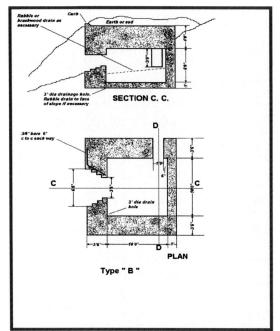

SECTION C. C.

PLAN

Type " B "

Most concrete constructions have been destroyed by modern British armies or lie buried beneath shifting sand dunes and vegetation, but there are still some indications of military activity. Short stretches of wire mesh held in place by steel pegs and rods show where once a road crossed the soft sand. Crumbling barbed wire can still be found perched on rusty steel spikes, which, once located, can by searching reveal a line or pattern of what was once a formidable obstacle to assaulting infantry.

Despite the most thorough ordnance clearing operation of Braunton Burrows in 1947, dangerous ammunition and mines are still being found so the reporting of suspicious objects with an accurate location is earnestly requested. Some areas are fenced off for livestock grazing experiments and these boundaries are to be respected. Prospecting with metal detectors is not tolerated and even possession of spent small arms ammunition is illegal as well as dangerous.

DOCTRINE

In 1943 no principle existed within the U.S. Army for assaulting a heavily fortified coastline, and the only published advice in an U.S. Army Field Manual was that assaulting troops should avoid such defences and take them from the rear.

The Assault Training Centre's assault doctrine had therefore begun from nothing. In May 1943 Thompson had called a month-long conference in London, seconding military experts from every service to thrash out a workable method of neutralising the German beach defences in western Europe. He called on speakers from experimental projects, collected vast amounts of data and photographs, and drew upon the combat experience of veterans of similar amphibious landings, including the raid on Dieppe.

Every aspect of the problem was considered, especially the terrain and topography to be encountered on the Normandy beaches selected for the American assault. This was probably the crucial element that dictated the whole doctrine, for unlike the British and Canadian assaults destined to cross sandy beaches onto undulating grasslands, the Americans would be faced with steep bluffs and only a few narrow valleys leading onto the plateau above.

While the British and Candians could therefore immediately use their tanks, the Americans had to seize the valleys leading off the beach first, leaving them no alternative but to attack the defences with infantry, and land their tanks once access off the beach had been secured.

Another factor that steered the conference to its conclusions was the lack of large landing craft, but a surplus of the humble LCVP. A thirty man capacity craft available in sufficient numbers, the LCVP proved to be the mainstay of the doctrine that was taking shape.

By the end of the month the doctrine was written together with a three week training schedule the conference concluded was necessary to adequately train soldiers in these new tactics.

A secret document of the time gives an appreciation of the problem and the American solution . . . "Modern fortified areas are characterized by a series of steel pillboxes, steel turrets, open emplacements, troop shelters, slit trenches and similar installations. Such defenses are commonly called Hedgehog.

The heart of the defensive system is the concrete and steel pillboxes. These are camouflaged, project only a small portion above the ground, and are so located as to provide interlocking zones of fire and mutual fire support. The entire area is surrounded by various anti-tank obstacles, ditches, tank traps, minefields, and from two to many bands of wire. The wire, minefields and normal avenues of approach for foot troops are liberally sewn with anti-personnel mines. The ground immediately before the weapon openings, or embrasures, in the pillboxes is levelled to provide long fields of fire. Where natural cover in the form of trees or underbrush is present, the trees and brush are cut down. Generally little, if any, natural cover for attacking troops exists.

The pillboxes have weapons that vary from machine guns to anti-tank guns up to light field artillery.

To successfully attack such a formidable area of new construction embodying the latest principles of modern tactics, infantry must be specifically trained, provided with additional weapons, and be backed up with a preponderance of artillery and direct fire weapons. In addition, air bombardment and ground support formations are extensively employed".

The technique for direct assault of such hedgehog fortifications to be taught at the Assault Training Center followed a general plan . . . " Infantry to be reorganized into assault sections; with flamethrowers and high explosive teams being the heart of the assault section. The troops advance under massed artillery and direct fire weapons preceded by an aerial bombardment, and covered by smoke. However, no reliance is placed upon actually reducing pillboxes by action other than direct assault.

The air and ground bombardments are relied upon to crater the area, spoiling the fields of fire and providing some cover, knock out the enemy artillery, destroy some of the open emplacements, and to cause the pillboxes to "button-up", thereby allowing the infantry assault sections to advance and close with the enemy.

Upon the close approach of the assault troops, the artillery lifts to the rear areas, preventing the enemy bringing up reinforcements. The direct fire weapons, normally anti-tank guns, tanks, tank destroyers and infantry cannon continue to fire directly on the embrasures until their fire is masked by the infantry. At this point the assault troops cover the advance of the flamethrowers and demolition teams with rifle, anti-tank, and bazooka fire. Wire cutting teams cut or blow the wire using Bangalore torpedoes. When the flamethrower and demolition men are within 40 to 60 yards of the embrasures, the flamethrower is fired at the embrasure to permit the demolition men to place their high explosives within the embrasure. In short, the demolition team are the "ball carriers". All other weapons and men are used to permit the demolition men to place their charges, thereby accomplishing the job of knocking out the pillbox.

Engineer troops closely follow the assault sections, and clear gaps thru the minefields, bridge anti-tank ditches and other tank obstacles to facilitate the forward movement of the track and wheeled vehicles. In most cases, Hedgehog are echeloned in depth. In other words there are successive bands of these positions, several hundred yards apart in depth depending upon the terrain".

Elements of the training programme were tested at Woolacombe by personnel of the 156th Infantry Regiment who were to be the instructors and guardians of the establishment. Only a few minor alterations were found necessary to individual lesson plans. The Assault Training Center was ready for their first trainees.

As the new doctrine drastically altered the conventional structure of an infantry division, the first problem to be encountered by the training staff was selling the idea to unit commanders. This was an issue that required diplomacy and rank to convince sceptical commanders that this was the way things had to be done, and the task fell to the Center's Executive Officer, Lieutenant Colonel Lucius P. Chase.

He pointed out that the U.S. Army found itself presented with a unique problem they had not encountered before. They were to assault a fortified coast - not merely a defended coast such as encountered in Sicily or North Africa. And this could only be solved by a unique remedy, stressing there was only a limited objective for their assault Divisions - to establish a beachhead then defend it against counter-attack. Most were quick to realise these objectives were limited because of the devastating casualties their Divisions were expected to bear.

The re-arrangement of their units was justified further when it was pointed out that with amphibious assaults there had to be more flexibility and decentralization than in land doctrine because uncertainty of reconnaissance of targets rendered detailed assignment of tasks impossible. This was furthered by the very great risk of sinkings and faulty navigation, and these anticipated losses had to be distributed among landing craft of the assault waves.

It was spelt out that the assault had to be made by specially equipped and trained infantry sections as direct fire could not be depended upon to reduce pillboxes, and normal infantry weapons were powerless against concrete. Therefore beach defences were to be blown by hand placed charges. This was to be done by self-contained thirty-man "Assault Sections" that didn't exist in conventional infantry divisions, and were the reason for re-structuring

Training therefore had to be based upon several assumptions. Firstly that pillboxes and gun emplacements must be neutralised by flat trajectory, high velocity gunfire. Naval firepower was expected to provide this, but confidence in this eventuality gradually waned with training experience and alternative methods of delivering this initial barrage were explored and integrated into the American assault plan for D-Day. Tanks and artillery firing from landing craft as they approached the shore was one idea adopted, backed up by a small force of DD Tanks.

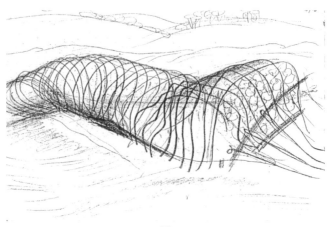

ASSAULT SECTION

This was the very backbone of the Assault Training Center's whole doctrine. It comprised of thirty infantrymen, divided into eight teams, each one trained in particular skills and together, practised to work as a self-contained unit.

Amphibious operations were new to nearly every soldier attending the Center, so alongside the usual safety regulations for waterborne operations, it was considered essential to give instruction on how to wear combat equipment while aboard landing craft, in the event they should find themselves in deep water and need to get rid of their equipment.

Training Memorandum ASLT – 18 listed what each soldier should carry, including :-

> Pack, field, less bed roll, meat can, knife, fork.
> 3 pkts "K" rations, to be carried in field pack
> 3 bars "D" ..   ..
> 5 (or 6) grenades, fragmentation and smoke.
> *96 rounds, M-1 ammunition to be carried in belt and bandolier.
> First Aid Packet, to be carried on belt.
> Canteen, cup, cover, on belt.
> Rifle, M-1
> Bayonet and Scabbard.
> Gas Mask to be carried as prescribed below:
>> Cover, protective, gas, to be carried in gas mask.
>> Ointment ..   ..

These articles are carried in the following manner until soldier reaches the beach:

a. The life belt is worn under the equipment. The pack is slung in the usual manner, with the exception that the cartridge belt is left unbuckled. The rifle is then slung over the left shoulder, sling to the front and muzzle up. The sling is then slipped over the bayonet hilt and around the canteen bottle. The gas mask is then placed on the top of the pack with long strap to the left. The strap is wrapped around the muzzle of the rifle and hooked onto the left front side of the cartridge belt. The short strap is brought directly over the right shoulder and fastened to the right side of the cartridge belt. The equipment is now secured to the belt and can be readily disposed of by a shrug of the shoulders in case of a fall into the water. The chin strap of the helmet is buckled at all times.

The Assault Section was ... " designed for frontal attack upon enemy fortified position, depending upon a system of coordinated fires to advance a highly specialized group to destroy the enemy fortifications. Enemy fires from other sources are neutralized by means within the section (mortar). The section is not designed for thorough mopping up but for breaching the enemy "crust" of defense".

ORGANIZATION : Each Assault Section is commanded by a lieutenant, who is the section leader; he is assisted by a sergeant, second in command of the section. The section itself consists of the following sub-teams; riflemen, wire-cutters, rocketeers, flame throwers, mortarmen, machine gunners, and demolition men

SUBTEAMS OF THE ASSAULT SECTION IN ACTION : The subteams of the assault section are organized and equipped to advance the demolition party to the vicinity of the pillbox, where it puts the pill-box out of action by placing explosive charges in vulnerable portions of the pill-box. The assault team is loaded into an LCVP (landing craft, vehicle and personnel) in a prescribed order which will permit the members of the team to debark in the following prescribed sequence:

The Section Leader
The riflemen   ...   .   (96 rds for M-1) (75 rds for carbine)
The light machine gun team   ...   (1500 rds)
The mortar team ...   .   (36 rds)
The wire cutting team
The rocket team ...   .   (36 rds)
The flame thrower team
The demolitions team

DEVELOPMENT UPON DEBARKATION : Immediately upon debarking covered by smoke from the chemical mortars firing from landing craft, the section leader and riflemen move straight to the front in a rough V formation with about ten yards interval and about five yard distance between riflemen. The light machine gun team and the mortar team deploy to the left in that order with similar intervals and distances, in

14

accordance with the procedure set forth in individual assault pamphlets. The wire cutting team, the flame throwing team and demolitions team initially deploy to the right in a similar fashion while the two launcher subteams deploy within the "V" about twenty yards apart and about twenty yards behind the section leader.

STEPS IN THE ASSAULT :
a. The section leader. Prior to the beaching of the landing craft, naval and aerial bombardment, have cratered the beach and full advantage of these shell and bomb craters is taken in the initial movements of the assault section. The assault section leader looks for the principal enemy fortification in his zone of action and for supporting enemy emplacements. He establishes communication with his supporting tank or gun by visual signal. He locates the elements of his assault section. Covered by the fire of the riflemen he moves forward locating possible points for breaching enemy obstacles, blind areas in the enemy fields of fire, etc. He causes routes to be marked out to these designated places by the riflemen, and he controls his section by prearranged signals, time schedules, phase signals, visual signals (usually arm and hand) and oral orders. The last two methods because of noise, smoke and difficulty of movement will be rarely successfully employed; emphasis must be laid on coordination of movement.

b. The assistant Leader. The assistant leader, a non-commissioned officer is the last man off the landing craft. He assists the section leader; is prepared to take the section leader's place, if the latter becomes a casualty; keep informed of the general situation at all times; and is particularly charged with the responsibility of locating covering fires from open emplacements and bringing mortar fire to bear upon such enemy installations.

c. The Light Machine Gun Team. The light machine gun squad takes position well to the flank of the assault section, where it can fire upon enemy installations taking care not to mask the fire of the supporting tank or gun. Should its fire be marked by advancing riflemen, the gun is moved to a new position from which the original target can be engaged. Short bursts of two or three rounds will be fired at the embrasure; however, the chief use of the machine gun will be in neutralizing fire from enemy open installations.

d. The Mortar Team. The mortar team moves to a position where it can bring fire on possible targets with maximum protection; they will receive orders from the assistant section leader to bring fire on open emplacements, but may direct fire on such emplacements at his own initiative. Fire is directed until the successful conclusion of the assault, when the mortar is prepared to fire on enemy concentrations and to break up enemy counterattacks.

e. The Rocket Launcher Team. The rocket launcher team moves up under the protecting fires of the riflemen, the machine gun and the accompanying tank until it reaches a position from which it can fire upon the embrasure. Rocketeers should take positions so that they are no nearer one another than twenty yards and where if possible communication can be established with the section leader. Fire is opened on the pillbox with armor piercing rockets to cover the advance of flamethrower and the demolitions party. When the flamethrower signals "I am ready", by arm and hand signal, the rocket fire is lifted. At the successful assault, the rocketeers advance to the next position or to attack a new pillbox as directed.

f. The Flame Thrower Team. The flame thrower team moves forward by short bounds, taking full advantage of cover, under the covering fires of the riflemen, the machine gun, the accompanying tank, and the rocket party until it reaches a point from which it can bring fire to bear upon the embrasure of the enemy pill-box. The assistant flame thrower keeps close contact with the demolition party, and when that party is in position to begin its assault, he signals to the rocketeer, "I am ready", by arm and hand or other pre-arranged signal, whereupon the rocket fire is lifted. The flame thrower party then opens with jets of one or two seconds and covers the placing of charges in the vulnerable points of the embrasure by the demolitions party.

g. The Demolitions party. Is "ball carrier" of the assault section for whom all the other teams do the "blocking". It works its way forward under the protective fires of the other weapons until it is ready to make the final movement to place the charges to destroy the pill-box. At this time, the leader of the party signals to the flame thrower party, "I am ready". The flame thrower then opens fire, and under the protecting jet, the demolition party places the necessary charge or charges in the vulnerable portions of the embrasure.

ASSAULT TRAINING CENTRE AREAS

Braunton Burrows - Training areas A,B,C & D

This vast expanse of sand dunes and slacks contained most of the live-firing ranges and dummy pillbox clusters where infantrymen were taught step-by-step, the individual tasks of each component of the "Assault Section". Here they practised from beginning to end the amphibious assault upon a heavily defended coast. From embarking onto

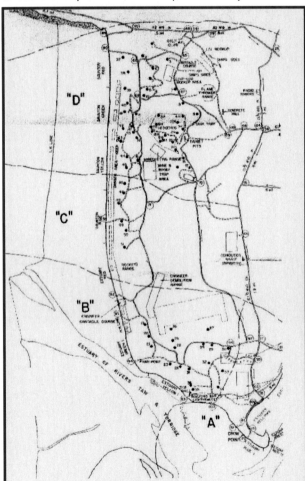

dummy landing craft, debarking, learning the skills of each Assault Section team, and finally attacking pillboxes as a co-ordinated unit.

By mid 1943 the Assault Training Center staff had already drawn up the training requirements for Assault Sections to ... " Learn proper methods of embarking in, debarking from, and wading ashore from landing craft, acquire individual skill in use of assault weapons, develop co-ordination of weapons in the assault, learn use of local smoke, methods of passing minefields and booby traps, and methods of crossing wire, develop fire-and-movement teamwork by an Assault Section in the assault of a defended obstacle, to include the reduction of a pillbox, practice co-ordination with adjacent sections, become accustomed to advancing under fire of supporting weapons, and co-ordinate movement with such fire".

AREA A

The most southern part of Braunton Burrows and the earliest area used with many training aids being abandoned in favour of larger versions in other areas. It contains many structures associated with elementary lessons of vessel embarkation and debarkation used prior to the troops first taste of riding in landing craft. It included the assembly and embarkation areas where men, vehicles and tanks were loaded onto landing carft supplied by the U.S. Navy based across the estuary at Instow.

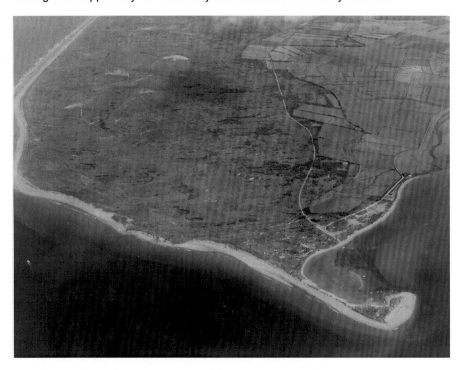

Constructions known to be in Area "A" :-

LCM/LCVP Mockup Area I   LCT mockups   Barge & Nets
Assembly Area   LCM Mockup Area II

Beaches:-   Estuary Blue I   Estuary Blue II   Estuary Yellow
              Estuary Green II   Estuary Red II

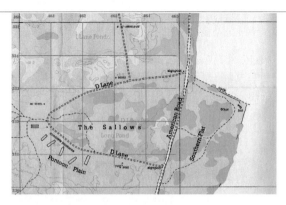

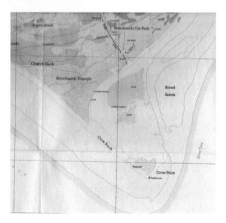

ATC Description	Grid reference	Remains found
LCT mockup	46122-33180	Commemorative plaque - Extra concrete apron at rear as Mk5 – Carved in wet concrete "146 ECB, Company C, 1st Platoon".
LCT mockup	46137-33146	
LCT mockup	46095-33190	demolished jaws
LCT mockup	46166-33080	overgrown
LCT mockup	46206-33082	demolished jaws
Concrete bases	45...-.3258	Many, blown, Assembly area
Concrete bases	45003-32560	Many, blown, Assembly area
LCM base	46335-33103	exposed
LCM base	46275-33120	partially covered

Sherman tank being reversed onto landing craft at Broadsands

21

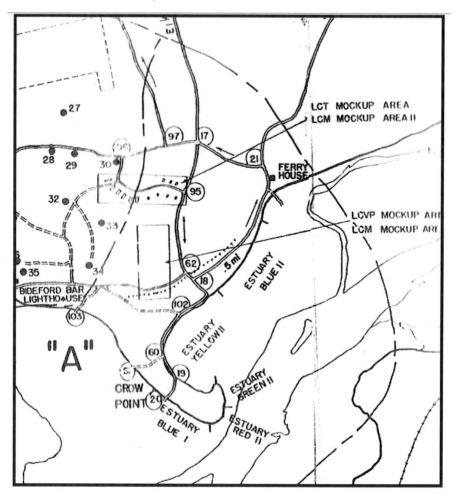

U.S. Army map – February 1944

Assembly Area :

All embarkations into landing craft, whether vehicles, tanks, artillery, or troops took place at various beaches around Crow Point. The U.S. Navy harboured their landing craft across the estuary at Instow, and Broadsands provided them with a sheltered loading area whatever the weather or state of the tide. Of necessity there was a Standard Operating Procedure for embarkation to handle the large number of troops involved.

The Beach Embarkation Officer had an office in a nissen hut at the dune line behind Crow Point where there was a telephone line and the microphone controlling the public address systems in the assembly and beach areas. The Beach Embarkation Officer would be notified by the Instructor or CO of the unit to be lifted, when . . . " the unit is ready for embarkation. Personnel to be embarked should proceed to the Assembly Area designated by the dotted lines, where they will find boat section numbers, black on white background, set on posts. The numbers are arranged so that the sections can move across the dune line after call for embarkation with no, or very little, lateral movement by the best routes of march. Occupation of the assembly area and movement to craft on beach should be in orderly fashion. Light discipline is in force if embarkation is during darkness. The unit to be lifted will designate a Unit Embarkation Officer who will work in close co-ordination with the Beach Embarkation Officer at the Beach Office. On call from the Beach Embarkation Officer the boat team guides will report and procure their boat team signs. The Beach Embarkation Officer will call for the boat teams loading when he has been notified to do so by the Naval Beachmaster. Boat Team numbers are carried aboard craft at embarkation and placed in upright position with number visible. On landing, boat team numbers are carried off the craft and left on the shore above the waterline".

1943 sketch of troops in assembly area

Concrete hut base in assembly area

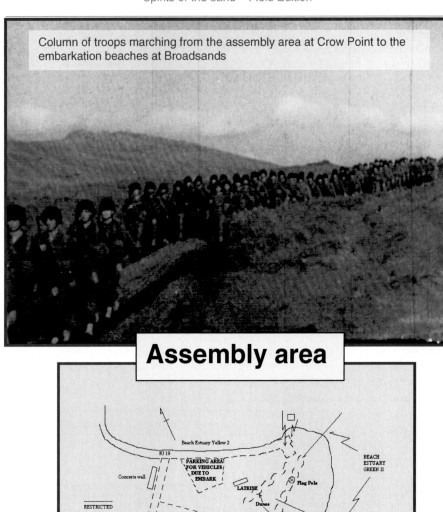

Column of troops marching from the assembly area at Crow Point to the embarkation beaches at Broadsands

Assembly area

LCM/LCVP Mockup area
Grid reference : 46335-33103
Description :   Concrete LCM base

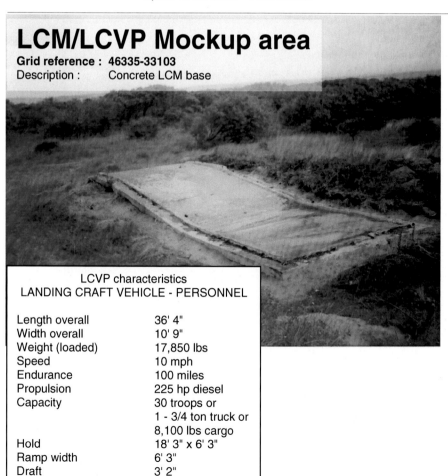

LCVP characteristics
LANDING CRAFT VEHICLE - PERSONNEL

Length overall	36' 4"
Width overall	10' 9"
Weight (loaded)	17,850 lbs
Speed	10 mph
Endurance	100 miles
Propulsion	225 hp diesel
Capacity	30 troops or
	1 - 3/4 ton truck or
	8,100 lbs cargo
Hold	18' 3" x 6' 3"
Ramp width	6' 3"
Draft	3' 2"

LCM/LCVP Mockup Area I

Located to the west of the "American Road" opposite Broadsands Car Park, the area measures almost 200 yards wide and 450 yards long. The "Boardwalk" cuts across the southern extremity and just to the north of this path is a recently uncovered flat concrete base that was probably a control hut for use by training staff. No surface evidence of any training mock-ups has been found - which were probably full-size concrete bases with wooden or corrugated sheeting superstructures. According to the 1943 lesson plan, this mock up area ... " simulates the boat waves afloat and its use familiarizes the troops with the positions of the craft in the (assault) formation. Its primary use is for training sections to take individual positions in craft and deploy therefrom".

LCT mock-up landing craft

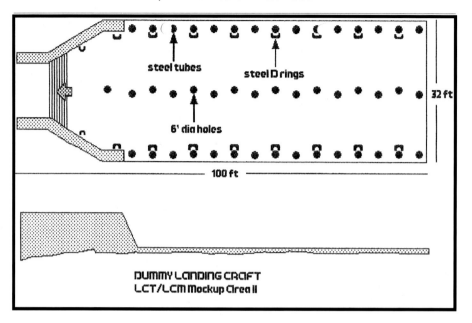

steel tubes

steel D rings

6' dia holes

32 ft

100 ft

DUMMY LANDING CRAFT
LCT/LCM Mockup Area II

LCT MOCKUP. BRIAN CHUGG 1947

Several of these large concrete part-replicas are still standing. Tanks, trucks and artillery would master embarking and debarking on these concrete bases that represent LCTs with lowered ramps - as if they had just beached.

Characteristics of LCT Mk 5 (Landing Craft Tank)		
Draft	3'1" forward	3'9" aft
Length overall	108' 0"	
Width overall	32' 0"	
Weight	124 tons	
Endurance	500 miles	
Propulsion	3 x 225 hp diesels	
Capacity	180 tons	
Ramp width	12' 6"	

The original bases were built to the dimensions of the Mk IV LCT, but as landing plans developed it became clear that the Mk V version would be used. Consequently additional aprons were added to the rear of existing bases to represent the extended deck area of the updated craft. Inscribed in wet concrete of one such extension is the mark of its constructors . . . " 146 ECB, Co C, 1st Platoon".

While only the bases, jaws and ramps of the LCTs are represented - evidence exists that six-foot high scaffold poles stood around the edges with probably canvas curtains hung between them to create the effect of the craft sides.

Barge & Nets

This area introduced troops to the most basic element of an amphibious assault, from scrambling over the side of a transport ship into landing craft and a short sea voyage. The Assault Training Center instruction guide AMPH W-2 & W-3 listed the equipment that was to be carried by the troops in training, including . . . " BARs, HMG, wire cutters, 81mm mortars, 60mm mortars, Flame Throwers, simulated pole charges, satchel charges and bangalores ".

The general plan was to spend forty minutes demonstrating how to properly wear their equipment and then assign groups to their individual mockups for an hour of practising embarkation and debarkation. After this they reassembled and moved to the beach at Estuary Red 2 and embarked on LCVPs and LCMs for a sea voyage to Croyde beach.

On arrival, they were to debark as practised, and advance inland . . . " assuming light resistance " for about three hundred yards.

A large wooden barge was grounded at the very tip of Crow Point, and although nothing today exists of this vessel, there have been some alarming finds of dummy hand grenades.

Here the lesson split the trainees into four groups, which rotated between a twenty-minute demonstration of how a 30-man section should descend using nets and lower their equipment. For an hour they practised this themselves, and then practised knots and lashings.

The first wave would then embark on landing craft for the sea voyage to Croyde beach.

Embarkation beaches

Estuary Blue II Beach:

Extends along the north shore of Broadsands from the White House - where an American made slipway still exists - almost to the beach access road from Broadsands car park. At the top of the beach are remains of a lateral concrete wall showing evidence of explosion damage.

Estuary Blue I Beach:

Running along the seaward side of Crow Neck to Crow Point - it has been totally eroded.

Estuary Yellow II Beach:

Continues anti-clockwise from its boundary with Estuary Blue II Beach, around the inside of Crow Neck to Crow Point. Most of this beach was covered to the low water mark with replicas of beach obstacles that would be found in Normandy.

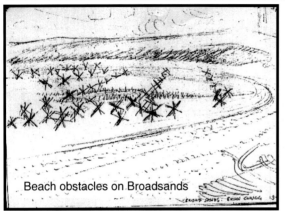

Beach obstacles on Broadsands

Estuary Green II Beach:

Was on the eastern side of Crow Point where . . . " all embarkation of vehicles on either LCMs or LCTs will take place, using the North portion of Estuary Red II Beach to the extent necessary. No vehicles are permitted on the beach except to be embarked".

On Friday 29th October 1943, First Lieutenant Gordon S. Ierardi - on a fact finding mission for the Adjutant General's Department - went to Crow Point and ... " witnessed the embarkation of troops and tanks in LCVPs and LCTs which were going to take part in an assault exercise on Woolacombe Beach that afternoon. These craft are manned by the Navy who have a base at Appledore. As is usually the case, many of the landing craft were stuck on the beach after taking on their cargo of men or vehicles and had to be pushed into the water by the Army DUKWs. A very interesting case of the Army having to put the Navy afloat !".

Estuary Red II Beach:

On the south eastern face of Crow Point, this was an alternative embarkation point to Estuary Green II Beach, and also a practice area for embarkation, when . . . " during instruction periods on the beaches, or barge, vehicles will be parked in the parking area denoted "Vehicles to Embark Only" and embarkation will take place on Estuary Red II Beach". This parking area was just to the northeast of the flagpole that still stands today.

Between Crow Point and the town of Appledore across the estuary was moored the USS "President Warfield". As a Chesapeake Bay steamer she had peacefully plied her trade of ferrying cars and passengers between small harbours along the Virginia shoreline until the summer of 1942.

Barry Dwyer, an American naval historian recalls her history ... " The U.S. War Shipping administration claimed her, and after modifications she sailed for England with seven other ex-coastwise steamers per request of the British Ministry of War Transport. They sailed on 21st September 1943 and most fell victim to U-boat attacks, but the "Warfield" came through unscathed. For her first few months in England she was moored at Instow, Devon, where, fast in the mud at low tide she served as a Combined Operations training and barracks ship. In July 1943 the ship was reclaimed by the United States and became U.S.S. "President Warfield" (IX-169). In April 1944 she was moved to Barry Roads to continue her training role as an assault boat training base, crossing the Channel on D+30 to serve as a station and accommodation ship for harbor control. In 1947 "Warfield" began transporting Jewish emigrants to Palestine having been renamed "Exodus" by her new owners, and starred in the book by Leon Uris and the subsequent cinema film".

AREA B

Occupying the south western part of Braunton Burrows, it contains the earliest constructions for assault training and a high proportion of unmarked and unidentified remains. One anomaly here is Churchill Plain - delineated as "out of bounds" to troops under training - it has yielded many finds indicating it was in fact used for assault exercises.

Constructions known to be in Area "B" :-

19	20	21	22	23	24	25	26	27
28	29	30	31	32	33	34	35	52

Engineer Obstacle Course   Engineer Demolition Range (part)

Beaches :-   **Estuary Yellow I**   **Estuary Green I**

Estuary Red (part)

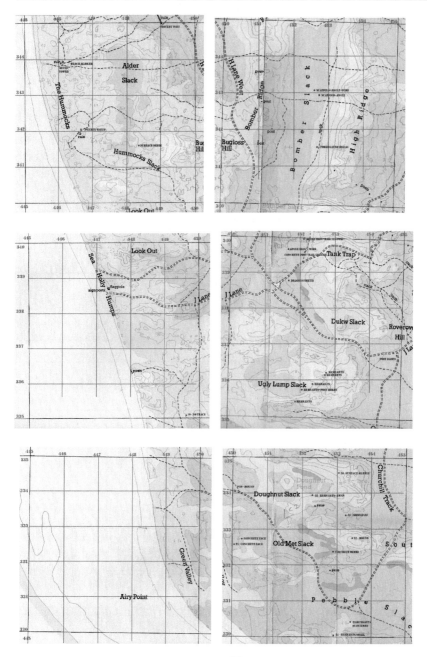

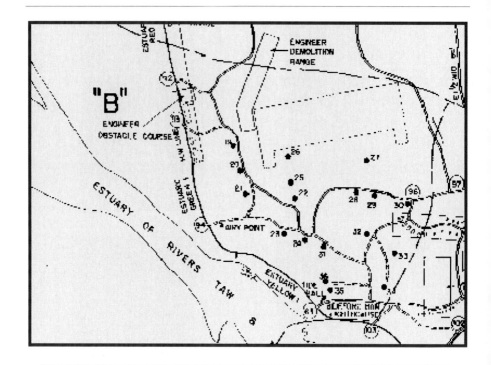

U.S. Army map – February 1944

Demolition charge on Dragon's tooth

Listed below are known ATC training aids and ranges, together with what remains have been located.

ATC Number	Grid reference	Remains located
19	44965-33509	No trace
20	45015-33420	Mound
21	45007-33259	Concrete face/rubble
22	45345-33276	Mound
23	45228-33042	Concrete remnants scattered
24	45295-33002	Concrete remnants small
25	45325-33340	Not located
26	45306-33458	Concrete surface rubble
27	46310-33490	Not located
28	45774-33325	Concrete + hedge + ditch
29	45777-33317	Concrete large debri
30	46080-33254	Single reinforcing bar
31	45538-32993	Concrete remnants small
32	45815-33045	Concrete surface rubble
33	45972-32907	Large remnants + steel
34	45925-32660	Not located
35	45885-32630	Not located
36	45512-32827	Surface ubble/cement/bitumen
52	45228-33398	Concrete remnants+BWSP
Assembly area	45820-32627	Single concrete base
Dragons teeth	45165-33878	Large concrete remnants
Engr Demo Rg	45216-33960	Concrete post + rail length
Engr Demo Rg	45266-34152	Metal corrugated zigzag
Engr Demo Rg	45166-33964	Metal fragments of angle iron
Engr Demo Rg	45211-33999	Metal Engr Demo Rg
Engr Obstacle Course		Not located

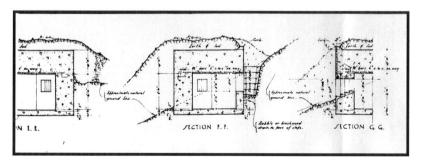

Other remains have been located and explored, yet remain unidentified from any maps of the Assault Training Centre, and it can only be assumed these were early constructions that were superseded by more sophisticated or useful constructions.

Description	Grid reference	Remains located
Pillbox	44665-34206	Demolished walls & base
	45776-33027	Concrete surface rubble
	45586-32720	MoD post
	44836-34163	Surface debri
	45234-33597	Scattered concrete remnants
	45187-33545	Scattered concrete remnants
	45272-33614	Concrete remnants
	45269-33612	Concrete remnants
BWSP	45235-33368	Barbed wire support post
Road junction markers	45203-33580	Concrete post bases
	45990-33795	Concrete base 6ft x 6ft
	45482-33668	2 x concrete post bases
	45612-33372	*Metal tanks (flamethrower)*
	46230-32627	*Single .303 1940 cartridge*
	45820-33505	Road wire *+ 2 inch mortars*
BWSP	45277-33188	Barbed wire support post
	45284-33239	Concrete debri
	45562-32693	Debri – pillbox configuration
	45745-33021	Surface concrete debri
	44602-34396	Metal observation tower
	44630-34398	Beach division marker

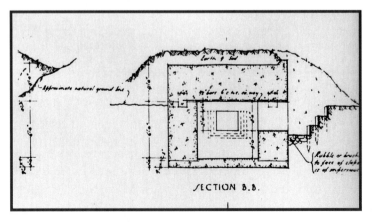

SECTION B.B.

Ranges 19 to 27

ATC Reference   Grid reference   Description

19	44965-33509	no trace
20	45015-33420	Mound
21	45007-33259	Concrete face/rubble
22	45345-33276	Mound
23	45228-33042	Concrete remnants
24	45295-33002	Concrete remnants small
25	45325-33340	NOT FOUND
26	45306-33458	Concrete surface rubble
27	46310-33490	NOT FOUND

Ranges 19,20 and 21:

It was known that barbed wire would be deployed as an outer defence to any fortification and it was essential to pass through this belt in order to attack the structure. Range 19 was used to teach and practice breaching these wire entanglements.

The lesson plan dated 1st November 1943, coded A-7, was taught to the Rifle team within each Assault Section and covered bridging and tunnelling of barbed wire.

The lesson was delivered to battalion sized groups who were first . . . " given a demonstration by School Troops on use of tracing tape. Companies will then be assigned one per range with each No. 1 Rifleman assuming active control of his party. Entire group of 30 will work toward barrier using creeping or crawling method of advance. One party will, as designated, cut gap with cutters, bridge it, or tunnel it. When one party has completed this performance, groups will rotate".

They were shown and practised alternative methods of approaching barbed wire, and once at the wire, how to pass over, or under it, or blow a gap, then mark their trail for following troops.

Assault Training Centre Reference # 28

Grid reference : 45774-33325

Assault Training Centre Reference : 28

All that remains of this training aid is a large mound with concrete debri on the surface. But the area surrounding 28 is intriguing as there is a long, deep ditch to one side that was probably a tank-run along the southern edge of Churchill Plain. Churchill Plain is shown on ATC maps as being "Out of bounds" but some most interesting finds have been made within the enclosure, including flame thrower bottles and mortar ammunition.

Ranges 29 to 52

Assault Training Centre Reference # 29

Grid reference :   45777-33317
Description :   Concrete large debri

Assault Training Centre Reference # 30

Grid reference :   46080-33254
Description :   Single reinforcing bar

Assault Training Centre Reference # 31

Grid reference :   45538-32993
Description :   Concrete remnants

Assault Training Centre Reference # 32

Grid reference :   45815-33045
Description :   Concrete surface rubble

Assault Training Centre Reference # 33

Grid reference :   45972-32907
Description :   Large concrete remnants + steel

Assault Training Centre Reference # 34

Grid reference :   45925-32660
Description :   NOT FOUND

Assault Training Centre Reference # 35

Grid reference :   45885-32630
Description :   NOT FOUND

Assault Training Centre Reference # 36

Grid reference :   45512-32827
Description :   Surface rubble/cement/bitumen

Assault Training Centre Reference # 52

Grid reference :   45228-33398
Description :   Concrete remnants+BWSP

ENGINEER DEMOLITION RANGE
ASSAULT TRAINING CENTER
CONSTRUCTED BY CO "A"
146 ENGINEER (C) BATTALION

REINFORCED CONCRETE DRAGONS TEETH

SECTION AA

Note: Each charge (▩) is 1/2 pack C-2.

SKETCH "B"

Dragons teeth

Grid reference : 45165-33878

43

Engineer Demolition Range

Excavation of part lateral line of obstacles across Bomber Slack

Assault Training Centre Reference : Engineer Demolition Range

Grid reference :   45216-33960
Description :   Concrete post + rail length

Grid reference :   45266-34152
Description :   Metal corrugated zigzag

Grid reference :   45166-33964
Description :   Metal fragments of
                      angle iron & wire

Grid reference :   45211-33999
Description :   Metal debri of angle
                      iron + lt rly track

Grid reference :   45271-34298
Description :   Scaffold & angle iron

The range ran the length of Bomber Slack - a perfect amphitheatre for explosions where the surrounding high bluffs formed a natural safety barrier for the constant demolition practice that went on here.

Evidence suggests that lateral lines of different obstacles stretched across Bomber Slack, compelling a progressive forward movement from the site of the "Dragons Teeth" north eastwards along the slack.

To the eastern side, evidence has been found of an observation post constructed of corrugated sheeting, probably reinforced with sandbags.

Grid reference :   45990-33795

Description :   Concrete base 6' x 6'
Use or purpose unknown – possibly base
for communications tower

Engineer Obstacle Course

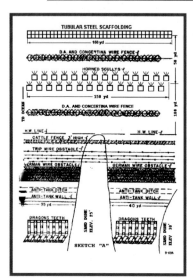

Major Reginald Page was … " in charge of the training of Engineer troops for the assault wave of the invasion, whose mission was the removal of obstacles to the landing of the main body. We had good intelligence from low-level aerial photography, and from personal scouting of the Normandy beaches by men landed from submarines . . . We got technical advice from the U.S. Chief of Engineers as to the quantity and placement of explosives".

Engineer troops would embark on landing craft at Crow Point for the short sea voyage to Estuary Red Beach where they would debark in the surf to assault the Obstacle Course. Working their way off the beach through the different belts of obstacles, their objective was to clear a path wide enough for a tank, for the entire depth of the course.

Good example of construction methods used.
This was an early type of dummy pillbox

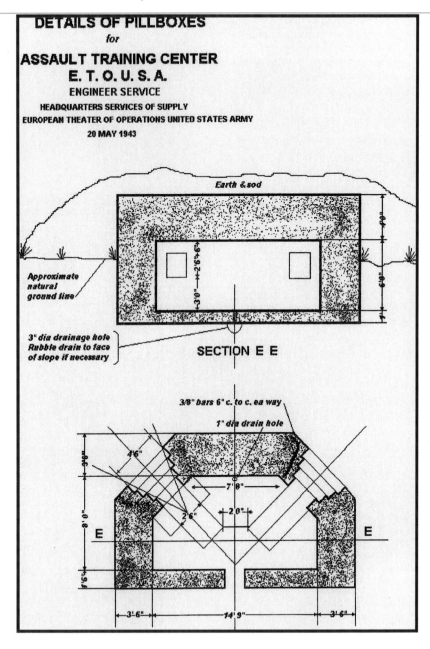

DETAILS OF PILLBOXES

for

ASSAULT TRAINING CENTER

E. T. O. U. S. A.

ENGINEER SERVICE

HEADQUARTERS SERVICES OF SUPPLY

EUROPEAN THEATER OF OPERATIONS UNITED STATES ARMY

20 MAY 1943

Earth & sod

Approximate
natural
ground line

3" dia drainage hole
Rubble drain to face
of slope if necessary

SECTION E E

3/8" bars 6" c. to c. ea way

1" dia drain hole

Grid reference : 45562-32693
Description : Concrete debri
suggesting pillbox configuration.
Not shown on US Army maps.

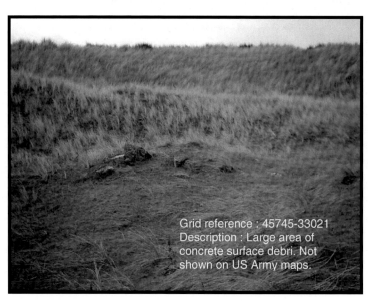

Grid reference : 45745-33021
Description : Large area of
concrete surface debri. Not
shown on US Army maps.

One of the more spectacular constructions lay on the shoreline of Area B. A wall of sandbags over twenty feet high and over two hundred yards long. Its use is unclear, is not marked on any maps and was probably experimental.

The Assault Training Centre's Diary Notes - 4th October 1943 . . . " Landing exercise held north of Airy Point. This is a hazardous area. One man was lost. The LCVPs are not doing well in the surf at the present stage of training of the crews. In this exercise there was decided congestion on the beaches. A naval beach party is needed and the junior officers should show more initiative in getting their units deployed and moved along. Colonel Thompson felt we were fortunate in not having more losses to date".

The 116th Regimental Combat Team of the 29th Infantry Division undertook this ill-fated exercise. They had planned it themselves based upon information provided by the Assault Training Centre for Field Exercise Number 3, where it was to be assumed that . . . " The western coast of DEVON is a section of the German held coast of NW FRANCE and the sector in which this exercise takes place is one of the more strongly defended sectors".

Their summary of enemy information was intimidating . . . " All pillboxes are surrounded by barbed wire, usually triple concertina with some double apron in evidence. This protective wire is generally about 50 yards from the pillbox or fortification. These pillboxes can usually be expected to be mutually supporting with interlocking bands of fire, which cover bands of tactical wire. They are also strongly defended by riflemen. The beach line has been heavily wired above the high water mark generally with two parallel bands of wire. Mines can be expected to be prevalent in the beach area above high tide, especially in the vicinity of the beach exits. The enemy is known to activate mines with booby traps and to make considerable use of trip wires. No evidence of underwater obstacles has been disclosed to date. The beach area can be expected to be heavily covered by both artillery and mortar fire. Latest estimates indicate that there are probably about two platoons of infantry manning the defenses in this sector. One Panzer division is located at EXETER, about 45 miles to the SE, and can close in the BARNSTAPLE BAY area by about H + 24".

For a touch of reality, a defending force was . . . " physically represented on the ground and will wear red hat bands".

Reality and safety had both to be considered. Live demolition charges were used, but blank ammunition was issued with strict orders that . . . " it will not be fired closer than 20 yds to personnel". And . . . " Physical contact between members of opposing forces is prohibited".

To ensure that all participants obtained the maximum training, casualties were not assessed, but . . . " In order to permit essential training of the battalion medical detachment with the landing team, designated personnel of the defending forces at each pillbox will, after the pillbox has been assaulted, be tagged by the umpire at the pillbox, the tag showing the type of wound. The tagged personnel will remove their red hatbands and remain in vicinity of the pill-box, and thereafter emulate and be considered as casualties of the landing team and will be treated and handled by the medical personnel of the landing team as such".

AREA C

Spans the whole central body of Braunton Burrows, but in 1943 the topography was predominantly flat and open, consequently the training ranges were concentrated in the coastal strip of dunes with pillbox-sized concrete structures running parallel to the shore.

A 30-man Infantry Assault Section – the basis of U.S. Army amphibious assault doctrine on D-Day.

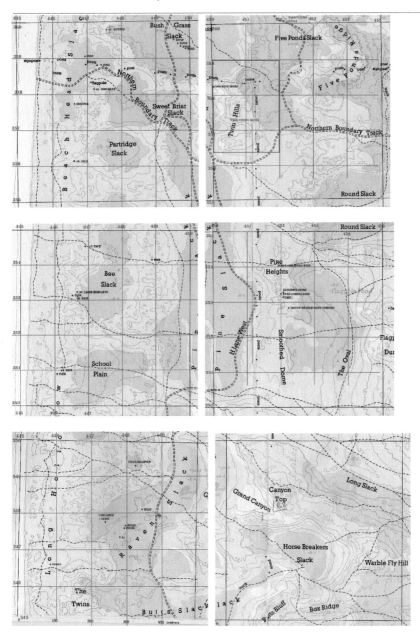

Constructions known to be in Area "C" :-

46   47   48   49   50   51

Engineer Demolition Range (part)   Rocket Range   Infantry Demolition Range

Beaches :-   **Saunton Blue**   **Estuary Red (part)**   **Saunton Yellow**

ATC Description	Grid reference	Remains found
46 ..	44660-35615	Concrete face
47 ..	44690-35454	Concrete face
48 ..	44667-35311	Concrete face
49 ..	44622-35106	Very large concrete blocks (face)
50 ..	44665-35323	Concrete face
51 ..	44777-34736	Large concrete remnants + steel
Rocket Wall ..	44990-34500	
Engr Demo Range	45258-34306	Pole + angle iron + wire stretch

| | **Unidentified & Contemporary relics** | |
Description	Grid reference	Remains located
	45777-34380	Roadtrack heap overgrown
	45232-35288	Mound + concrete rubble + sawn timbers
	44843-34810	Section of "American road"
Track markers	44790-34762	Scaffold pole stumps
Track markers	44794-34764	Scaffold pole stumps
BWSP ..	45061-36071	Many - possibly dump
Beach marker	44630-34398	Steel triangle atop pole
Obs tower	44602-34396	Metal construction
	44592-34632	Rubble & scree
Collapsed pits	44800-34900	Contain steel,timber,vehicle parts

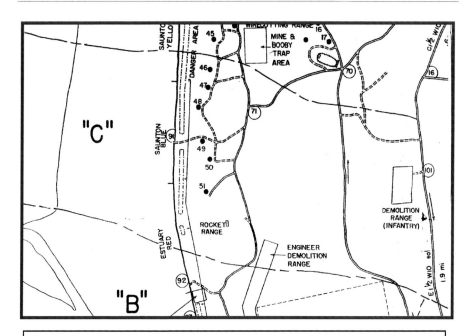

U.S. Army map February 1944

"Ships Sides" – Scaffold structure for training troops to embark into LCVPs from the mother ship down cargo nets.

Assault Training Centre # 46

Grid reference :   44660-35615
Description :   **Concrete face**

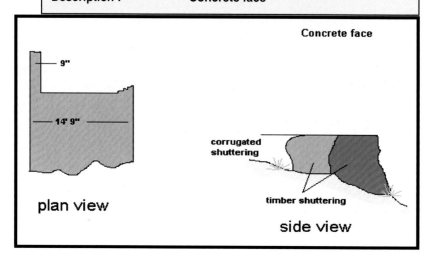

Concrete face

9"

14' 9"

plan view

corrugated
shuttering

timber shuttering

side view

Assault Training Centre # 48

Grid reference :   44667-35311
Description :   Concrete face

Assault Sections spent a lot of their training time at these faces and pillbox dummies using live ammunition in practice assaults for an hour at a time. Their assault runs were always to seaward, generally perpendicular to the barbed wire perimeter, and invariably encountered anti-personnel mines and booby traps deliberately placed by training staff, just to add that touch of realism. However, safety took precedence over realism when mortars were used – they had to aim at concrete blocks way behind the pillbox being attacked. More than one assault section took part at these sites so one could carry out its assault while the other took instruction on how to deal with anti-personnel mines and booby traps.

Typical dummy pillbox

Assault Training Centre # 49

Grid reference :   44622-35106
Description :   Demolished concrete face

Typical concrete "face"

Assault Training Centre # 50

Grid reference :   44665-35323
Description :   Concrete face

Assault Training Centre # 51

Grid reference :
44777-34736
Description :   Large
concrete remains + steel

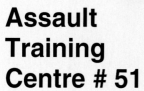

Assault Training Centre :
Rocket Wall

Grid reference :   44990-34500
Description :   Large concrete remains + steel

Bazooka Team of an Assault Section

Bazookas were such a new weapon to the U.S. Army they didn't have time to publish a manual on its specification, limitations or tactical uses before the Assault Training Center got to hear about it. They were quick to recognise the weapon's potential for their own specialised needs, and soon incorporated it within the Assault Section.

Situated in Butts Slack the concrete wall was a target backdrop for rockets being fired from the floor of the slack beyond H Lane West. Here, contrasts in vegetation colour indicate foxholes and trenches used by the marksmen. Many Bazooka heads and fins have been found at the base of the wall, and nearby steel wreckage suggest whole vehicles were also used as targets in front of the wall.

| Grid reference : | 45777-34380 |
| Description : | Steel roadway |

Nearly all the trackways laid by the U.S. Army have now been removed, although there are several complete examples still remaining in isolated areas.

Their method of construction was, after grading the route, to lay bitumen sheeting with an open steel mesh on top. This mesh was then secured laterally, and along the edges with steel strips securely pegged along the entire length.

These trackways were of adequate width to take a six wheeled truck, and strong enough to carry all the heavy construction vehicles necessary to maintain the training aids.

Observation tower
Grid reference : 44602-34396
Description: Metal construction

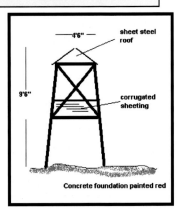

4'6" — sheet steel roof

9'6"

corrugated sheeting

Concrete foundation painted red

Grid reference :   45232-35288

Description : Mound + concrete slabs + sawn timbers

Explosive store for Mine & Booby trap area

Beach markers

Grid reference : 44630-34398

Description : Steel triangle atop steel pole

Assault Training Centre : Infantry Demolition Range

This large, flat area ran for some 300 yards beside the American Road from just south of Sandy Lane Car Park, and extended 100 yards west across Hog Wood Plain. Here the Demolition teams of five infantrymen learned and practised their new skills, starting from basic charge preparation through to constructing the specialised explosive packs they would use to subdue enemy fortifications. Everything depended upon their ability to successfully conclude the assault on an enemy fortification, and they were especially selected from the ranks as being already proficient in their basic arms of carbine and hand grenade and judged to be level headed and reliable under fire.

As they gained confidence in handling explosives, specialised charges were introduced to their lessons. The Pole Charge - consisted of about ten pounds or more of TNT packaged on the end of a pole 8 or more feet in length and fitted with primer and fuse lighter. The time fuse was cut shorter than usual to ensure firing before the enemy could dislodge the charge. The Satchel or Pack Charge was much like the Pole Charge but without the pole and comprised of a TNT charge packaged or taped to a board with a rope handle.

It was known that to breach a 6-foot thick pillbox wall of reinforced concrete required around 400 pounds of explosive, so the demolition parties hand placed charges went for the weak points. The embrasures, door hinges and locks, and other weak spots such as angles in roof and walls. It was recognised too that while a breach may not be made by the first charge, the concussion inside the fortification may temporarily neutralise the occupants long enough for a second charge to be placed.

The Demolition Party had their own detailed instructions when landing . . . " to advance as fast as possible behind the wire-cutting, Bazooka and flame thrower parties. When the objective is within range of the rocket launchers, all demolition men with the exception of one or two will remain under cover. The flamethrower party advances on signal, closely followed by one or two demolition men prepared to assist or even replace the flamethrower in case of necessity. The remainder of the party may follow in echelon. After the embrasure engaged has been forced to close up under the fire of the flame thrower, the first demolition man runs forward, in a blind spot, and places his first charge, pulls the fuse lighters, and dodges to the nearest cover. After a breach has been made, the occupants may be more fully liquidated by a satchel charge or hand grenade thrown into the breach".

AREA "D"

The northern part of Braunton Burrows contained the greatest concentration and diversity of assault ranges and training constructions. The majority were built on Saunton Golf Course, and have long been demolished or lie buried beneath greens and fairways.

Constructions known to be in Area "D" :-

1	2	3	4	5	6	7	8	9
10	11	12	13	14	15	16	17	37
38	39	40	41	42	43	44	45	

Flamethrower range   Concrete wall   Tank trap   Target pits
Wirecutting range   Mine & booby trap area   Radio towers
LCVP/LCM mockup area   Obstacle course LCI mockup   Shipsides
Hedgehog

Beaches :-   Saunton Green   Saunton Yellow   Saunton Red

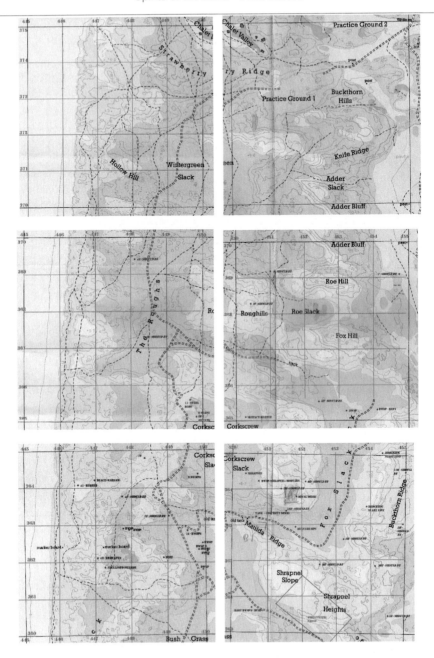

ATC Number	Grid reference	Remains located
1	.. .. ..	Not located
2	.. .. ..	Not located
3	.. .. ..	Not located
4	.. .. ..	Not located
5	.. .. ..	Not located
6	.. .. ..	Not located
7	.. .. ..	Not located
8	.. .. ..	Not located
9	.. .. ..	Not located
10	.. ..	Not located
11 ..	44965-36560	Steel reinforcing bars
12 ..	44885-36491	Mound
14 ..	44953-36290	BWSP
15 ..	44951-35954	BWSP
17 ..	45582-35768	Concrete slabs
41 ..	44650-36407	Concrete rubble
43 ..	44705-36211	Concrete remnants/large block
44 ..	44754-35981	Concrete rubble
45 ..	44721-35814	Concrete remnants + scree
Hedgehog North perimeter	45323-36528	BWSP
6H ..	45189-36412	Scree + shrapnel + wire
7H ..	4.5185-36381	Metal debri + shapes
	45389-36350	Phase 2 start line North/South ridge
	45435-36502	Phase 2 start line North/South ridge
Flamethrower Range	.. ..	Not located
Obstacle Course ..	.. ..	Not located
Wirecutting Range		
Tank Trap	.. .. ..	Not located
Mine & Booby trap Area		
Radio Towers ..	.. ..	Not located
LCVP/LCM Mockup area ..	..	Not located
LCI Mockup	.. .. ..	Not located
Shipsides	.. .. ..	Not located

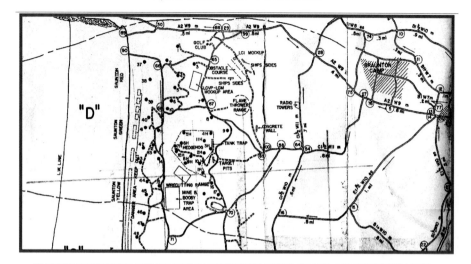

U.S. Army map February 1944

Assault section advancing

Unidentified & Contemporary relics

Description	Grid reference	Remains located
Tank + concrete debri ..	45069-36324	Matilda tank
BWSP (many)	45407-36531	
Explosive store	45207-35323	Concrete slabs + timbers
Observation post	45200-35323	Metal tube + corrugated
BWSP	44775-36294	
BWSP	44792-36295	
Formed concrete debri ..	45002-35826	
Concrete bases	4625-3585	Within treeline
Mounds	44980-36510	Seven in North/South line
BWSP	44964-35944	
BWSP	44972-35935	
Barbed wire	44988-35930	
Tank shell head	44988-35932	
Concrete post	44891-35414	
MoD post	44890-36213	
MoD post	44740-35884	
MoD post	44693-35905	
BWSP	44997-36255	
BWSP	45001-36246	
BWSP	45004-36239	
BWSP	45008-36225	
Concrete & stone debri.. ..	44988-36237	
Collapsed pillbox	44724-36188	
Dog tag	Howard W KNIGHT - 0.885740 – T43 A P	
Sleepers + iron bolts ..	44663-35776	
Concrete construction spoil	46208-35722	
Anti tank wall	Saunton Golf Course - east side of 14 on West course	
Pillbox (whole!)	Saunton Golf Course - 13th green on West course	
Concrete hut base ..	Saunton Golf Course - west end of clubhouse	
Concrete hut bases ..	Saunton Golf Club - demolished on fairway just SW of clubhouse	
Pillbox or face	Saunton Golf Club - between fairways	

Machine gun team in action

Assault Training Centre # 11

Grid reference :   44965-36560
Description :   Steel reinforcing bars

ATC # 12

Grid reference :   44885 - 36491
Description :   Mound

ATC # 13

Grid reference : 44905 - 36325
Description : Mound

ATC # 14

Grid reference : 44953-36290
Description : BWSP

Assault Training Centre # 15

Grid reference :   44951-35954
Description :   BWSP

Assault Training Centre # 17

Grid reference :   45582-35768
Description :   Concrete walls collapsed outwards

ATC Reference : Range # 40

Used for mortar instruction, starting with lessons in identifying ther component parts of the weapon, ammunition functions, and sighting on open targets.

88 mm Mortar crew in action

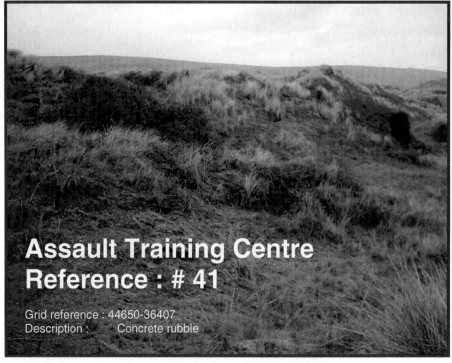

Assault Training Centre
Reference : # 41

Grid reference : 44650-36407
Description :   Concrete rubble

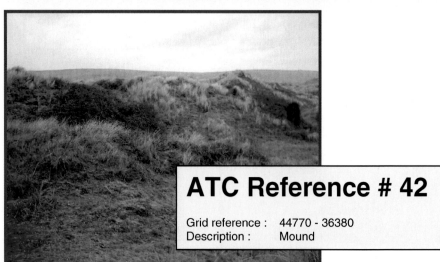

ATC Reference # 42

Grid reference :   44770 - 36380
Description :   Mound

Assault Training Centre # 43

Grid reference :   44705-36211
Description :   Concrete remnants / large block

Assault Training Centre # 44

Grid reference :   44754-35981
Description :   Concrete rubble + corrugated shuttering

Assault Training Centre # 45

Grid reference : 44721-35814
Description :   Concrete remnants + scree

Assault Training Centre :
LCI Mockup

This has disappeared altogether, being in the middle of a golf club fairway, southeast of Practice Ground 3.

ATC Ship sides
Three huge scaffold towers, draped with cargo nets where troops practised their descent into landing craft.

Assault Training Centre : Obstacle Course

800 yards long, stretching over sand dunes in the shape of a horseshoe, travelling south taking a semicircular turn to the right and heading North so that the beginning and end of the course are only 100 yards apart. The course is ten yards wide and is run in teams of five abreast. Designed to acquaint soldiers with

OBSTACLE No. 1 & 8: Concrete wall (one foot thick, nine feet high and 30 feet long) comparable to tide or beach walls on French beaches.

OBSTACLE No. 2: Barbed wire net (30' x 30', 18" above ground level, stretched over a 30' x 30' x 3' deep hole) Its purpose is to attempt to teach men to crawl through trenches and to move swiftly in a crouched position to afford as small a target as possible.

OBSTACLE No. 3: An overhead ladder (width of the course and 18' long and 8' above ground level, over a ditch, four feet deep, filled with barbed wire. Cross bars are spaced 18" apart and run across course.)

OBSTACLE No. 4: Ditch (width of course and nine feet across, six feet deep and filled with barbed wire.) Confidence jump.

OBSTACLE No. 5: Hurdles (four feet high, across course. Three in number.) Simulates brick wall and fences that have to be crossed in street warfare.

OBSTACLES 6,12 and 15: Concertina wire (3 wire rolls stretched across course 12" above ground.) Teaches men the proper method of crawling under wire to be cut and at same time teaches them to keep low on the skyline.

OBSTACLE No. 7: Balance logs over concertina wire (Five logs nine inches in diameter, 18' long.) Balance Test.

OBSTACLE No. 9 and 11: Confidence Jump (Jump, nine feet down over barbed wire.)

OBSTACLE No. 10: Cable Walk (2 parallel cables stretched across thirty foot ditch, one cable directly above second cable. 6'6" apart.) Balance, arm and confidence exercise.

OBSTACLE No. 13: Combination ship ladder and cargo net. Presents two devices that personnel will run across on board transport, ship ladders from hold to deck and cargo net over side.

OBSTACLE No.14: Swinging Bridge. (Cable bridge with wood flooring.) Balance test.

OBSTACLE No. 16: Rope Swing. (8' rope hanging from 12' crossbar, over a 4' ditch.) Arm and stomach exercise.

OBSTACLE No. 17: Bear Trap. (Wire entanglements knee high.) Keeps the soldier foot conscious and wary of trip wires.

OBSTACLE No. 18: Sand bag wall. (5 foot high with ditch behind four feet wide and filled with barbed wire.) Tiresome jump after ½ mile of running.

OBSTACLE No. 19: Balance Walk. (Zig-zag walk through barbed wire.) Balance test after the ½ mile trip.

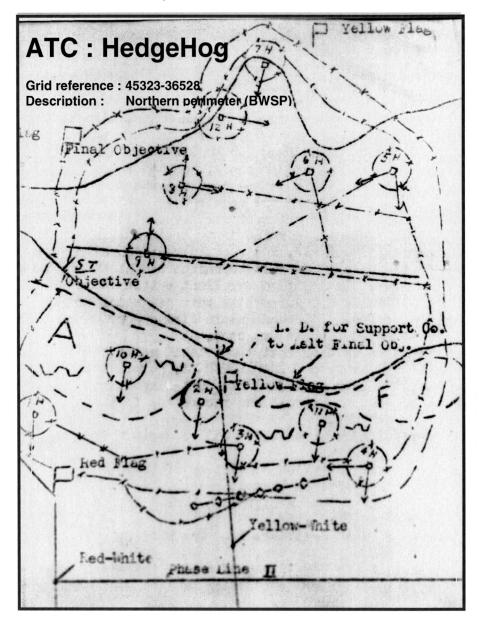

ATC : HedgeHog

Grid reference : 45323-36528
Description : **Northern perimeter (BWSP)**

Assault Training Centre : Hedgehog

Pillbox clusters				
1 H	2 H	3 H	4 H	5 H
6H	Grid reference : 45189-36412		Scree + shrapnel + wire	
7 H	Grid reference : 45185-36381		Metal debri + concrete shapes	
8 H	9 H	10H	11H	12H

Start line Grid reference : 45389-36350 to 45435-36502

**Assault Training Centre
Flamethrower range**

Saunton beaches

Assault Training Centre
Wirecutting range

Sleepers + iron bolts
Grid reference: 44663 - 35776

Bunker, wall & causeway

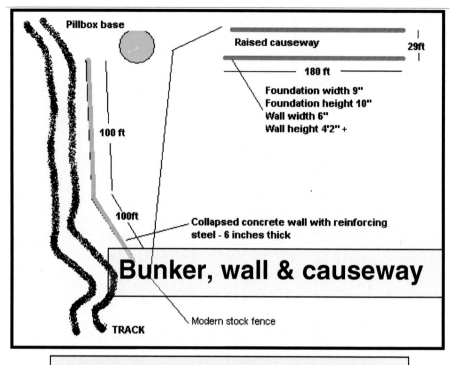

Pillbox base

Raised causeway

29ft

180 ft

Foundation width 9"
Foundation height 10"
Wall width 6"
Wall height 4'2" +

100 ft

100ft

Collapsed concrete wall with reinforcing
steel - 6 inches thick

Bunker, wall & causeway

Modern stock fence

TRACK

Series of mounds

Grid reference :   44980-36510   in North/South line
44985-36439   Nine mounds

AREA "E"

Croyde Bay was principally a tented encampment for troops under training, with officers billeted in the holiday camp chalets. The bay was used for practice DUKW landings and elementary amphibious exercises.

ug202 Croyde Bay from the Down

Facilities known to be in Area "E" :-

Croyde Camp: - Tent city situated in the dunes behind the beach. Nothing remains today.

Croyde Hall - Lectures and critiques for junior and senior officers took place here, but the original building has been demolished and replaced by a more modern structure on the same site.

Croyde Yellow II Beach Was the entire beach of Croyde Bay. This, with the dunes immediately behind were used for practice landings and DUKW exercises in ferrying men, supplioes and artillery ashore. There still remains an American constructed slipway for DUKWs at at the north end of the bay, off the road that leads to the National Trust car park.

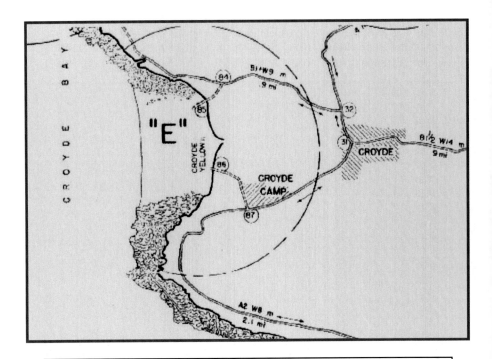

U.S. Army map – February 1944

AREA "F"

Baggy Point was a late addition to the Assault Training Centre's training areas as a need for Company sized rehearsals was identified. Some of the original farm banks and hedges were removed and the gaps can still be seen today. Also in situ are three huge concrete blocks – identical to those found on Braunton Burrows – each representing an enemy pillbox. Behind the main training area are several smaller training "faces". Fingered into the wet concrete of one is the name, A.A. Augustine. His unit was responsible for many of the constructions in the Assault Training Center, and landed ahead of the infantry on the enemy shore. Private Alfred A. Augustine, Company B, 146th Engineer Combat Battalion was killed in action on Omaha Beach on D-Day.

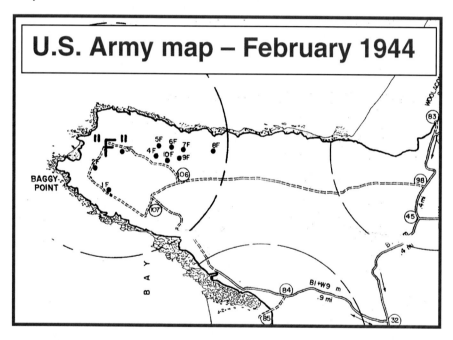

U.S. Army map – February 1944

Constructions known to be in Area "F"								
1F	2F	3F	4F	5F	6F	7F	8F	9F
10F								
	Observation House			Troop shelter				

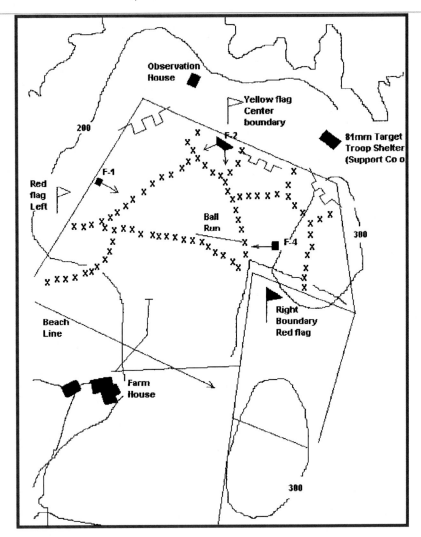

In 1997 the National Trust, headed by Shirley Blaylock, undertook a detailed historic landscape survey, which was published late in 1999. In it the National Trust recognises the significance of these remains by grading them as being of "Regional importance". They admit that . . . " three of the structures (6F, 9F and 10F) were destroyed by the National Trust some time ago before there was a recognition that concrete structures from WW II were of historical and archaeological value", but now recommend that . . . " surviving dummy pillboxes and associated earthworks should be retained as features of national interest".

The **Observation House** only exists today as a low sandy mound with some mortared brickwork protruding above ground. The **Troop Shelter** was never a construction, just a wall of sandbags along the rim of a disused quarry on the cliff top.

There were uses for the cliffs of Baggy Point too. Some of which aroused the interest of the tough American Ranger Battalions, the British COPP units that carried out covert reconnaissance raids on the German held Channel coast, the secret American OSS, and the U.S. Navy raiders.

The Assault Training Center Diary Notes for 22nd October 1943 explains their pioneering work that had drawn them to attention . . . " The practice of landing small groups by rubber boats in odd places has been sufficiently successful, to lead, to the attempt to make a much more important factor of it. It is referred to as "Infiltration Landings". In several of the early trials he (Captain Melody) made successful landings on the rocks of Baggy Point.

About the first of September 1943, a "raider" section of one officer and 29 men was set up for specialized training in raider tactics and techniques. Subjects stressed were:

The mission was to land on rocky shores, inaccessible to ordinary craft and establish a small bridgehead. The experiment was so successful that an infantry company is now being trained in these tactics. The ultimate aim is to make this nucleus of a larger group which will land on an unfavorable - hence weakly defended coast, and establish a strong bridgehead which will neutralize enemy coast artillery fire on the assault troops on the beaches. Note that the concept has departed from that of raiding in its usual sense. These forces, to be known as infiltration troops, are not to be hit and run - but to hold on to what they seize till the main force can take over. In this point they resemble airborne units and are in fact, intended to be used in conjunction with them. They carry enough supplies for 48 to 72 hours - counting on resupply over the beaches or by air as the situation permits".

   a. Handling rubber boats, particularly in surf.
   b. Cliff scaling.
   c. Forced marches.
   d. Hand-to-hand combat.
   e. Night operations.

Baggy Point was a useful area into which training grounds could expand as the Centers' Diary Notes for 13th November 1943 record . . . " A new type of exercise has been added to our training which is that of the assault company. It was found that there was too great a gap from the training in individual and team assault to the complete battalion exercise. The company exercises are held in the Baggy Point area and live ammunition is used".

Situated on top of the headland, these ten pillbox structures formed a self-contained practice and battlefield area. Each time it was used, agreement had first to be reached with the Coast Guard to vacate his lookout post.

Code A-23 - "Company in the assault of a fortified beach" was the new exercise drawn up with a scenario when . . . " the area on Baggy Point is assumed to be a portion of the German held coast of Northwest Europe. It is part of "Red Beach", which is assumed to be approximately 1200 yards long. The water line is marked on the ground by a line of white and yellow poles. Pillboxes and open emplacements are manned, but enemy reserves have been temporarily immobilized by preparatory bombardment and our paratroops. The strength of the garrison of Red Beach is unknown, but is estimated to be a reinforced platoon.

Your battalion has been ordered to make a daylight landing on Red Beach, assault and overcome the beach defenses and push inland to seize the battalion objective. The battalion is landing with two companies in the assault wave, your company on the left. Four 4.2 inch chemical mortars under battalion control, will lay smoke from H-5 to H Hour.

Your company, with 8 M-4 tanks attached, will assault the beach defenses on its front, seize the beach exit and cover the landing of the support company".

AREA "G"

Woolacombe Blue Beach:

This is really Putsborough and was the southernmost of the Woolacombe coded beaches. It was little used by the Americans except for small-scale landings or specialised cliff-climbing exercises. There was a strongpoint of concrete pillboxes and machine gun posts on the cliffs, and was one of the objectives of larger scale landing exercises further north on Woolacombe Sands.

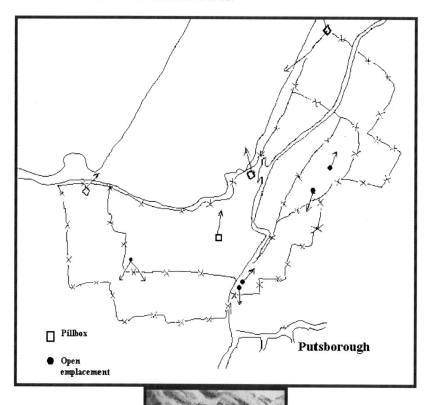

□ Pillbox

● Open
emplacement

Putsborough

AREA "H"

Woolacombe Sands was divided into four beaches. Blue Beach was at Putsborough, and Red Beach was directly in front of the town. Green Beach and Yellow Beach were the two main destinations for full-scale amphibious assault landings once the troops had mastered and practiced their new tactics.

The area of flat sand and scrub immediately behind the beach and below what is now Marine Drive was divided, chequer board style, into small exercise areas, each containing different types of obstacles that engineers and infantry would encounter on the enemy shore. It was here the engineers learned and practised their demolition, mine-laying and mine-removal techniques.

The Assault Training Centre Diary of 23rd October 1943 notes that . . . " the first formal landing exercise on Woolacombe sands was made by School Troops. Colonel Thompson was first American to step ashore. The inexperienced troops were enthusiastic and did well. The navy personnel handled the craft well in the surf"

On Thursday 28th October 1943, Lieutenant Gordon S Ierardi . . . " accompanied and witnessed an assault attack on Woolacombe beach by five infantry companies who landed from DUKWs. Saw the loading and rode with the men into the assault onto the beach.

As explained to me by Colonel Ely, the purpose of the attack was to hold the captured bridgehead and the hills back of the beach. The group attacking the left flank were to be held up while the two groups attacking the center and the right flank were to be permitted to reach the top of the hills, which were their objectives. If the center companies gain the top of their hill and then swing off and encircle the left hill, relieving the left companies who are under fire from the hill, and thus permitting them to advance, the problem is a success and the attackers have won. If the center attackers reach the top of their hill, hold it, and maintain a strong reserve, the problem is considered a draw. If the center attackers achieve the top of their height and then swing away off to the right or continue their advance forward, it is assumed that the whole attacking force would be split and the beachhead lost. The attacking force followed the correct course and the problem was adjudged in their favor. The unit which carried out this exercise was the 2nd Battalion of the 116th Infantry".

This was Field Exercise #1 and assaulting formations were given detailed information in order to plan for their attack which, unknown to them, was already looking like the real invasion plan. The attackers were to assume that a Ranger battalion had seized the high ground on their flanks and destroyed fixed guns that threatened their landing. The British forces were to their left, and their landing was to be in daylight.

Realism was added too by the presence of School Troops at the "enemy" fortifications - and they had their orders too. They were allowed a generous amount of blank ammunition for machine gun and anti-tank weapons, and instructed to loose off parachute flares in order to confuse signals of the landing force as well as laying trip wires connected to small sticks of explosive in the barbed wire.

AREA "L"

This area included one little used landing beach, "Woolacombe Red" that was too dangerous for amphibious assault landings because of its proximity to the rocks. The Assault Training Centre's headquarters was based in the Woolacombe Bay Hotel, and the town itself played host to many officers billeted in the local houses.

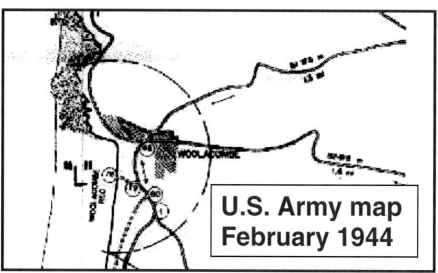

U.S. Army map February 1944

Woolacombe Red Beach

On the northern end of Woolacombe Sands, it was little used for specific landings, more as a buffer zone for craft that were swept off their designated landing spots further south on Woolacombe Beaches Green and Yellow.

Assault Training Centre Memorial

Situated below the road to Mortehoe, on the cliffs overlooking the length of Woolacombe Sands, the memorial was dedicated in May 1992 by Brigadier General Paul W. Thompson.

The inscription reads :

"On the sixth of June 1944 three Allied armies - British, Canadian and American invaded the continent of Europe over the heavily fortified beaches of Normandy - It was the greatest amphibious assault in military history and was a decisive battle of World War II - In the autumn of 1943 the United States Army Assault Training Centre was established at Woolacombe with headquarters in the village and encompassed Woolacombe and Saunton Sands their adjacent hinterlands and the sea approaches - This memorial is dedicated to those thousands of American soldiers whose preparation on the sands of Woolacombe and Saunton in the months preceding D-Day carried them to glorious victory on the sands of Normandy."

Woolacombe Bay Hotel

Requisitioned as the Assault Training Centre's headquarters in 1943, the hotel still stands, now sheltering a bronze plaque in the entrance lobby to commemorate the American wartime presence, and a group photograph of long forgotten soldiers.

First Lieutenant Robert O. Coll was posted to the U.S. Assault Training Centre to be Assistant Personnel Officer . . . " One night I was Officer of the day, and at about 3.00 am the phone rang. Did I know a Captain Peckham ? Cautiously I said yes. All of our activities were so secret that I hardly knew what to say. Well, the MP, I presume, said that he had been found drowned in one of the enormous water containers, perhaps fifty feet square, that were in London for fire fighting. Obtaining his phone number I awakened Colonel Metheny - Executive Officer, to deliver the message. Was this an accident or sabotage? I never heard any more".

Another strange and unrecorded happening was witnessed by Lieutenant Coll when . . . " one evening a small plane, fighter - U.S. I believe, crashed in the sea very close to the pounding waves on the rocky coast, to the west of the beach and lawn in front of the Bay Hotel. I think the pilot was rescued".

AREA "M"

Morte Point formed the most northern practical boundary of the Assault Training Centre and the promontory was used as a target for sea borne artillery cruising off Woolacombe Sands.

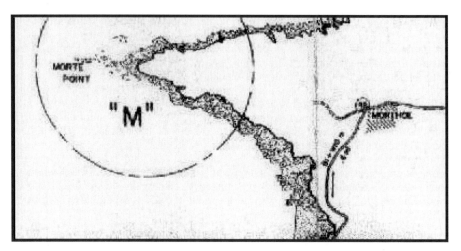

Major Russell T. Finn joined the Assault Training Centre staff in early 1943, and was appointed head of artillery. He was almost immediately confronted by the problem of supplementing direct fire onto enemy fortifications as the assault waves closed on the shore. And he came up with an ingenious scheme. He remembers . . . " To the best of my knowledge artillery had never before been fired from landing craft. The ATC experimented with the idea and had a partial solution. The difficulty with firing land based artillery pieces from landing craft is the lack of a stable platform. The two requisites, direction and distance (range) are the same whether on land or sea. The landing craft can be moved in the general direction of the target and the range can be determined with range finders on the craft. The range is normally set on the cannon by means of levelling a bubble. The solution we used was for the range finder operator to continuously call out ranges. The range setter on the weapon would set the ranges and the gunner responsible for firing would watch the range bubble, and when centred, would fire".

The Assault Training Centre Diary Notes record that . . . " On 21st September 1943 artillery was fired from landing craft for the first time at the Assault Training Center, and for the first time in ETO. Battery "A" 224th F.A. 29th Division furnished the materiel and personnel. The battery was loaded aboard an LCT5 at Crow Point and moved out to the vicinity of Baggy Point. The target range was located on Morte Point. Ranges of 5,000 yards and less were fired".

On 24th January 1944 the Assault Training Centre Diary Notes had to add . . . " In connection with firing weapons from craft it is interesting to note that the artillery officers of the RCT's that come for training are generally very dubious when they hear of it, and are surprised by the successful results".

The initial experiment had used two types of artillery piece for comparison. Towed howitzers and self propelled guns of the same calibre. The four towed 105mm howitzers were loaded onto an LCT-5 with their prime movers, one ammunition truck and three jeeps. The self-propelled battery was divided with three howitzers on each of two LCT-5's.

Chains with turnbuckles were used to secure the howitzers to the craft. Wheeled vehicles were chocked and blocked, and no difficulties were experienced with the howitzers moving due to recoil, nor did any loads shift due to rough seas.

Their target on Morte Point was a two hundred yard square subdivided into four one hundred yard squares. Data taken at the time shows that accuracy on the smaller target was between 34 and 45 percent, and on the larger 200 yard target, accuracy more than doubled, giving Major Finn the optimism to quote that an accuracy of 60 per cent was achievable.

Encouraged by their initial success, and continuing the tradition of the Assault Training Center of innovation, experiments were conducted in firing the 155mm self-propelled gun from an LCT. The conclusions were that it was as accurate as the smaller 105m field pieces, but to justify its use in the early waves it would need to hit individual pillboxes. Something that could not be guaranteed. The Assault Training Center Diary Notes of 14th November 1943 observed that . . . " Owing to its flat trajectory, "lost overs", when firing on Morte Point were a cause of considerable concern to the range officer". There is no record of the 155mm gun being used afloat on D-Day.

OTHER AREAS OF INTEREST

Braunton camp

Some American constructions and achievements in the area can still be seen. Alongside Challoners Road in Braunton is a concrete water-collecting tank. Here water was taken from the River Caen and pumped over the hill to a huge reservoir at the back of what is now Saunton Park. Around this estate some of the original concrete roads of the hutted camp still serve as public access to the homes, which now stand where nissen huts once housed American troops.

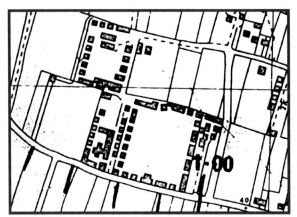

In late 1943 with winter closing in, it was considered unreasonable that troops should live under canvas, and there was concern that more permanent facilities should be available as the Center's Diary Notes on 13th October 1943 . . . " Colonel Thompson inspected the work of the 398th Engineers. Braunton Camp is 65% complete (350 out of 505 huts), and should be ready by the end of October. Next RCT, the 115th, will occupy it instead of tents. Further projects of the 398 Engineers are mess halls and showers at Ilfracombe and storage facilities at the Mortehoe Station".

Sure enough, the weather worsened, construction difficulties multiplied, the need for Braunton Camp became more urgent, and now Colonel Thompson took a personal interest as the Centre's Diary Notes show on 31st October 1943 . . . " Colonel Thompson conferred with Colonel Wyman concerning forthcoming occupation of Braunton camp (on 5 and 6 November by 115th RCT). Was assured that camp would be ready for occupancy by that date".

By 4th November it was noted that things had worsened yet again . . ." Seriousness of mud situation. Roads rough through the area and are deteriorating during the wet weather. Mud is becoming the number one problem. The Braunton camp is a sea of mud and utilities are far from complete. It was decided to quarter the artillery battalion and one infantry battalion of the 115th RCT in the tent camps".

Colonel Thompson was becoming frustrated by 9th November . . . " The Braunton hut camp is still decidedly deficient in all mechanical equipment and services. The sewage system is doubtful and the roads are definitely inadequate. Colonel Thompson felt alternative camp facilities had better be available for the next RCT and made provisions to move tents to dry sandy areas".

On 3rd December 1943 . . . " Colonel Thompson inspected Braunton camp with Major Douglas (398th Engineer General service Regiment), and found roads and drainage greatly improved. A great deal of rock has been used and the heavy part of this work should be finished in about three days. Thirty trucks are in use, hauling a total of six to seven hundred loads daily".

Mortehoe Station

The railway line from Barnstaple to Ilfracombe has been torn up in many places, but Mortehoe Station still exists with some wartime storage buildings nearby. Further down the line, Braunton car park stands on the site of the railway station where long troop trains had to pull forward three or four times to allow all American soldiers to alight on the country platform.

Instow

The U.S. Navy took over the entire foreshore to beach and dry out their landing craft after use in the Assault Training Center's amphibious exercises at Woolacombe and Saunton. There was a small camp at the eastern end of the beach that was used for repair and maintenance, and a slipway for their DUKWs which is still in use today for the very same purpose. Carved into a stone wall alongside this slipway are a few names of the local Home Guard who patrolled the shoreline.

Exploratory excavations have been made among the dunes following local reports of buildings being buried there, but no evidence was found to substantiate this, apart from a concrete base of a nissen hut.

Fremington

Today the camp is owned by the British Army and is the headquarters for all training ranges in North Devon including Braunton Burrows.

In January 1944 the camp was taken over by the U.S. 313rd Station hospital with approximately 300 enlisted men, 70 commissioned female nurses and about 40 medical officers, half of whom were administrative staff. The hospital remained at Fremington throughout 1944 and when re-designated as the 827th Convalescent Center, moved to a U.S. Army camp near Andover, Hampshire.

On the 31st of July 1944 the … " Body of 2 Lt J.B. attached to 45 Replacement Battalion US Army, Braunton, Devon found on Saunton Sands approx 8.30 am. Deceased had been bathing at Saunton Sands on 30 Jul 44 with other officers but had not been reported as missing. Body identified by 2nd Lt Alexander E Woodside of same unit. Body removed to Braunton mortuary and later to 313 American Field Station Hospital at Fremington, Devon. Buried at Cambridge American Cemetery".

VISITORS

There was a never ending queue of visitors to the Assault Training Center from the very day of its opening. Military personnel were professionally intrigued by what was happening here, and it was a showcase of American military might, proudly exhibited to diplomats, politicians, and military "top brass". But even by 30th September 1943 as the Centre's Diary Notes . . . " Unofficial 'observers' and hangers-on are to be eliminated in future".

The Assault Training Centre took official action as was noted on the 14th October . . . " It has become evident that this organization has become a center of attraction for high ranking officers and officials of both nations. As a result of this and other factors the office of Headquarters commandant was set up, one of its functions being that of Visitors Bureau".

Lieutenant General Gerow, commanding general of V Corps visited the Centre on 23rd October 1943. Afterwards he commented that he wanted to see . . . " more extensive umpiring and was critical of the U.S. Navy's too cautious restrictions".

Media interest was intense and although the press were made welcome to what was a "secret" establishment, they were closely chaperoned around carefully selected activities. On 31st October 1943 . . . " received large (46 in number) delegation of press representatives. Day passed very successfully all representatives agreeing that day was very much worthwhile. They were impressed especially with precise organization of their schedule".

Individual visits of high ranking officers continued as well as informal visits by staff from the British Combined Operations Experimental Warfare Station at Westward Ho, on the other side of the estuary.

Then came one of the two most important inspection visits of all. Just about every unit commander of the Allied invasion force was to descend in one party on 19th November 1943. For security reasons they travelled in two separate trains from London.

Their schedule of events opened with a brief introduction to the assault Training Centre, and then a description of what they would be seeing . . . " All events on today's program are normal training schedule items. Troops concerned are chiefly elements of the 115th RCT of 29th Infantry Division. Troops have been at Center 10 days and will remain 7 days more. First 9 days have been devoted to individual and small-unit training; today's schedule marks start of training on battalion scale. Training period ends with a regimental landing-assault exercise".

The top brass were then escorted around the Assault Training Center in a long, winding convoy of jeeps, and parked finally in Woolacombe to watch an assault landing on Woolacombe Sands.

On 12th January 1944, another very important party arrived. This time a group of Russian officers were given the grand tour of the Centre, perhaps as a politically supportive gesture to the British and American promise to Stalin of opening the "Second Front". Witnessing the activities and objectives of the Assault Training centre would hopefully convince the Russians of the sincerity of that promise. Their only recorded comment was . . . " Where are the supporting aircraft ?"

Between 1st October 1943 and 31st January 1944, which represents most of the Centre's working life, it played host to 805 official visitors - all of whom were high ranking military officers of the Allied nations, all keen to see what the Americans had devised.

Admiral Wilkes watches a dawn assault landing

CASUALTIES

Considering the vast number of troops involved in live-fire exercises, and the realism of battle added by instructors, it is a tribute to the safety rules imposed by the Assault Training Center that the casualty rate for troops under training was not much higher.

Invariably casualties were the result of some unforeseen circumstances or complete accidents. As Lieutenant Ierardi reported that in the week prior to his arrival on 26th October 1943 . . . " A most unfortunate accident occurred. While troops were being trained to advance under machine gun fire, one of the guns either went out of control or lost the correct range, firing into a group of men, killing five and wounding fourteen. On Saturdays Hedgehog, another couple were hurt. An inexperienced 57mm gun crew went completely haywire and fired a shot into one of the houses of the little village of Croyde from the training area. In every week there are several casualties, but this is the price which must be paid for this most valuable training".

He continued . . . " The training undertaken at the Assault Training Center is taken most seriously and at times is definitely hazardous. Training with live ammunition presents a real problem. The problems (exercises) must be intense enough to acquaint the participating troops with actual battle conditions and indicate to them proper methods of self-defense but on the other hand, they must not be so intense as to frighten the individual soldier and injure his fighting spirit. The Center makes every effort to achieve this goal and I believe that they achieve their aim. However occasional violent accidents are unavoidable".

A frequent visitor to North Devon, Mr C. remembers . . . " When in 1947 I first visited Woolacombe I remember seeing a bronze plaque fixed to the wall - now the car park - about 10" by 12". This plaque commemorated 98 U.S. Army personnel who were drowned in Woolacombe Bay whilst preparing for the D-Day landings. To our horror some years later we discovered it was missing, only to think that it had been bulldozed into the ground on enlargement of the car park".

An eye witness account, perhaps of the same event is given by Mrs H . . . " At the time that training took place for the coming invasion of Europe in 1944, I lived with my mother in Mortehoe and worked in the "Red Barn" café near the beach. I can recall one day helping my mother to give first aid to many who had been recovered from the sea when barges were overturned and sank. The café was used as a rescue station and I can remember the floor being covered with troops needing resuscitation and that many lives were lost that day".

A similar tragedy is recalled by Major Pixton who . . . " was unable to be on the beach as the initial waves were coming ashore, but was in my office on the third floor of the headquarters hotel, the office facing the beach. I looked out the window to see the waves of landing craft approaching the beach. Off to my right were three landing craft by themselves which were much too far to the north of the beach area and were heading directly for the rocks. The landing craft were LCMs, which were designed for carrying a tank, a truck, a couple of jeeps, or personnel. Each of these three LCMs was carrying a tank. They waited until they were close to the rocks before they took any action. Then as if by command all three of them turned to their right toward the sandy part of the beach area. By then they were inside the line of breaking waves. The minute I saw them I yelled at an assistant who was in the office to bring me my chest waders immediately. As I was putting them on I was watching the three landing craft and the inevitable happened. Because the surf waves were big that day, and the landing craft were travelling parallel to the waves, all three of them capsized. I ran to the beach to help in any way possible, but there was nothing which could be done at that time. The tide was in and the surf was heavy. We had to wait until the tide receded before we could do anything. There were fourteen men killed that day in that incident, nine soldier tank crewmen and five Navy landing craft crewmen. I personally pulled nine drowned tank crewmen out through the turrets of the three tanks. Lifting that dead weight was extremely difficult. We also had to turn over the upside down landing craft so they could be recovered and removed. That was the most physically exhausting day of my life, as well as the emotional strain which accompanies such incidents. To my knowledge that was the single most costly training accident we ever had at the training center".

1..LASSIFIED PER EXECUTIVE ORDER 12356, SECTION 3.3, 74500I

By *VSW/RB* NARA, Date *7/31/87*.

28 Oct. 43

During the Hedge-Hog exercise the following unusual incidents occurred. A 57mm AT shell hit the building of the Duke of York School going through some walls. No one was injured. A British training plane fell into the sea about 2000 yards out beyond the firing area. Two RAF officers, one Group Capt. Chilter of Chivenor Airdrome, parachuted down and were rescued by DUKWs.

Gun positions are to be selected with great care and safety rules carefully followed.

Colonel Thompson resumed conferences with Maj.General Lloyd C. Brown, CG, 28th Infantry Division. Arranged with General Brown details of schedules by which his RCT will be trained. Arranged for Cadre of Division to report here on 6 November. General Brown concluded the facilities of the Center are admirably adapted to completing the training of his Division, particularly in assault phases of the landing operation. General Brown stated he would proceed to org- anize his battalion at present station, to conform with our doctrine.

Staff List

Albright Capt Chester H.   0369187   MC   Surgeon, Special Staff
                              *promoted Major and Chief, Medical Sec, Stn Complement
Anderson 1st Lt Charles L.   Inf   Serv Co 156th Inf, Claims Officer
Arnold Capt Robert M.   SC   Signal Section, Assault

Bach Maj Stanley K.   Inf   Infantry Section, Assault
Bailey Capt Joseph S.   Inf   Supporting Section, Amphibious
Bamford Capt Warren H.   CE   Engineer Section, Assault
Baray Capt Robert R.   CE   Range Section, Training
Barber 1st Lt Donald P.   Inf   S-1 Section, Station Complement
Barbour 1st Lt Paul H. Jr   MC   Medical Sec, Station Complement
Barysh Maj Noah   MC   Chief, Medical Section, Assault
Baxter Lt Col Charles E. Jr   QMC   Chief, Supply & Construction
Bayless Capt William G.   Inf   Chief, Intelligence Section
Beacock 2d Lt Lewis E. Jr   0422326   Inf
Beatson Capt John B.   GAC   Chief, Anti-Aircraft Section, Trng
Betsen 2nd Lt Casper F.   Inf   Range Section, Training
Boseman Maj William A.   Inf   Tactical Exercises, Assault
Boyle 1st Lt Charles E.   CE   Infiltration Section, Amphibious
Brewster Lt Col Myles W.   017597   GSC   Chief, Doctrine & Development
Brewster Maj John P.   FA   Artillery Section, Assault
Bright 2nd Lt Eugene W.   FA   Assistant Adjutant, Special Staff

Calhoun Capt Howard O.   Inf   Anti-Tank Co 156th Inf   Air Defense
Campagna 2nd Lt Joseph R.   FA   Artillery Section, Assault
Campbell Capt John A.   CE   Engineer Section, Assault
Campbell Capt Laurie P.   Inf   Co A 156th Inf   Dep Fire Marshal
Campbell WOJG Bobbie O.   USA   S-4 Section, Station Complement
Cauble Maj Gordon B.   SC   Signal Officer, Special Staff
                              *promoted to Chief, Signal Section, Assault
Chaney Capt Edgar L. Jr   Inf   Serv Co 156th Inf, Munitions
Chase Col Lucius P.   Inf   Chief, Training
Coll 2nd Lt Robert O.   FA   S-1 Section, Station Complement
Culley 1st Lt Charles C.   SC   Chief, Photography Section
Curry Capt Charles L.   CE   Supporting Section, Amphibious

Daigle 1st Lt L. E.   Inf   Attached, Infantry Section, Assault
Dann Capt Daniel I.   MC   Medical Section, Assault
Day Col Alfred C.   CWS   Chief, Chmcl Section, Amphibious
De Kruyff Lt Col Richard D.   CE   Supporting Section, Amphibious
Dervas 1st Lt James   CE   Engineer Section, Assault
Deutsch Lt Col Albert   Inf   Doctrine & Development
Dobbins Maj S.O.H.   CE   Hq Commandant, Special Staff
Doyle Pvt John T.   3216819
Drislane 2d Lt James J.   01578397QMC
                              *promoted to 1st Lt and Chief, S-1 Sec, Station Complement

Echols Capt Eugene S.   CE   Supporting Section, Amphibious
Elias 2nd Lt Albert J.   CE   Supporting Section, Amphibious

Elliott 1st Lt Frank A.	CE	Infantry Section, Assault
Ely Col Louis B.	FA	Director, Amphibious
Ernest 1st Lt Herbert M.	DC	Medical Sec, Station Complement
Finn Lt Col Russell T.	FA	Chief, Artillery Section, Assault
Fakleman 2nd Lt Joseph J.	Inf	Attached, Infantry Section, Assault
Friesz 1st Lt L. O.	Inf	Attached, Infantry Section, Assault
Gamble 2nd Lt Julian B.	Inf	Attached, Infantry Section, Assault
Gillan WOJG Patrick J.	USA	Hq Co 156th Inf, Asst Comm
Gillespie Lt Col R.L.	Inf	Chief, Administration
Gordon 1st Sgt Harry	20714920	
Haas Lt Col George A.	Inf	Inspector, Special Staff
Hacker 2nd Lt Alex A.	CE	Infantry Section, Assault
Hackett Maj A. J.	FA	Artillery Section, Assault
Hall Capt DeWitt N.	Inf	Chief, Range Section, Training
Hawkins 1st Lt Malcolm	Inf	Assault Section, Amphibious
Heikkila Capt Frank E.	SC	Signal Section, Assault
Heywood Capt Alba S.	Inf	S-2, School Troops
Holliday Maj Joseph A.	Inf	S-4, School Troops
Hoppough 2nd Lt Robert L.	NHB	Asst, S-1 Sec, Station Complement
Horton Col John B.	FA	Director, Assault
Hoskin 2nd Lt Richard K.	SC	Signal Section, Assault
Houston Lt Col Earl P.	CE	Chief, Supporting Section, Amph
Hubbard 2nd Lt L. V.	Inf	Infiltration Section, Amphibious
Hunter Capt Robert F.	CE	Supply & Construction
Jobes Maj James G.	CE	XO, Supply & Construction
Karczewski Pvt John J.	35170230	
Kaufman 2d Lt Jonah	0178689 QMC	
Kelley 1st Lt Russell J.	Inf	S-4 Sec, Stn Cmplment
		*kia 27th July 1944 with 23rd Inf Regt, buried Colleville
Kennedy Maj Charles E.	CE	XO, Doctrine & Development
King 1st Lt Samuel C.	CMP	Provost Marshal, Special Staff
Kleeb 1st Lt Roderick E.	0408696 AGD	
Kunzig Lt Col William B.	Inf	Chief, Tactical Exercises, Assault
La Iacona 1st Lt Salvatore	Inf	Assault Section, Amphibious
Lard 1st Lt Arthur D.	Inf	S-4 Section, Station Complement
Laycock 2nd Lt R. A.	Inf	Infiltration Section, Amphibious
Learnard Lt Col Henry G. Jr	Inf	Tactical Exercises, Assault
Lewis 2nd Lt Joseph A.	CE	Infantry Section, Assault
Lock Col E.P. Jr	CE	Chief, Operations
Ludlow 1st Lt Kenneth C.	Inf	Attached, Infantry Section, Assault
Mango Maj Albert E.	MC	Medical Sec, Station Complement
Mathewson 1st Lt John I.	Cav	Infiltration Section, Amphibious
		Kia 26th April 1944 on Exercise Tiger
Maxfield Capt Alcee F.	Inf	Chief, S-2 & S-3 Sec, Stn Cmplment
McCaleb Lt Col Albert F.	Inf	Special Services Officer
McCrackin Capt Edward D.	CE	Infantry Section, Assault

McKenna Capt R. A.	FA	Artillery Section, Assault
McWhorter Maj William H.	AC	Chief, Air Section, Assault
		*departed 19th October 1943
Melody Capt Philip E.	CE	Chief, Infiltration Section, Amp
Metheny Lt Col L.C.	FA	Executive Officer, Operations
Miller Capt Marcel V.	TC	Supply & Construction
Miller Lt Col H. A.	FA	Executive Officer, Training
Moore Maj Elzie K.	Inf	Chief, Infantry Section, Assault
Moore 2nd Lt William J.	CE	Infantry Section, Assault
Morrison 2nd Lt Eugene L.	Inf	Attached, Infantry Section, Assault
Murphy Capt Thomas J.	0320267	Inf
		*promoted to Major and Chief, Tank Section, Assault
Murphy Capt Thomas E.	CE	Supply & Construction
Nachand 2nd Lt E. G.	Inf	Attached, Infantry Section, Assault
		*kia 13th June 1944 with 8th Inf Regt, buried Colleville
Nowak 1st Lt Charles E.	Inf	Hq Co 156th Inf,Comm Officer
Olin 2nd Lt Harold G.	Inf	Assistant Hq Commandant
Page Maj Reginald J.B.	CE	Chief, Engineer Section, Assault
Palmer Capt Mac A.	0401497	Inf
		*promoted to Major, Supporting Section, Amphibious
Petty Capt Frank E.	Inf	Assistant Special Services Officer
Pewinski 2nd Lt F. P.	Inf	Attached, Infantry Section, Assault
Pixton Maj Allan G.	FA	Executive Officer, Amphibious
Pointer Capt Jesse C.	FA	Artillery Section, Assault
Raymond 1st Lt James I.	FA	Chief, Library
Riley 1st Lt Edwin H.	Inf	Navy Liaison Section, Amphibious
Ritchey Capt Dan A. Jr	Inf	Adjutant, School Troops
Robbins 1st Lt Alex	Inf	S-4 Section, Station Complement
Roten Capt Charles T.	Inf	Doctrine & Development
Sargent 2nd Lt Donald	CE	Range Section, Training
Sawyer 1st Lt L. F.	FA	Artillery Section, Assault
Schattenburg Maj Gus A.	Cav	Supply & Construction
Schoenbeck 1st Lt Earle C.	Cav	Supply & Construction
Schneider 2nd Lt H.F.	Inf	Range Section, Training
Seawell 1st Lt Walter W.	SC	Signal Section, Assault
Shock 2nd Lt Hobert E.	Inf	Attached, Infantry Section, Assault
Short 2d Lt David M.	01579109QMC	
		*promoted to 1st Lt and X O, Station Complement
Sibert 1st Lt Ray S.	Inf	Transportation Section
Siverson Lt Col A. G.		Chief, Navy Liaison Section, Amphibious
Smith Capt A. T.	Inf	Tactical Exercises, Assault
Smith 1st Lt B.P.	Inf	Training
Smith 2nd Lt Elmore R.	CE	Navy Liaison Section, Amphibious
Smith Capt Spencer D.	PC	Finance Officer, Special Staff
Smith Maj Stanley K.	Inf	C O, Station Complement
Smith 1st Lt Stephen J.	Inf	Chief, Transportation Section
Smith 1st Lt Victor J.	Inf	Chief, S-4 Sec, Station Complement
Stahl 2nd Lt John	AGD	553rd APO Unit, Postal Officer

Stangler 1st Lt Harvey E.	Inf	Co A 156th Inf	EM Mess Officer
Stephens Maj Ralph	Inf	Training	
Stevens 1st Lt Charles H.	Inf	Co A 156th Inf	Off Mess Officer
Swan Capt Casimir J.	SC	Signal Section, Assault	
Switzer Maj Frank C.	Inf	S-3, School Troops	

Taber 1st Lt Charles S.		AG	Library
Thompson Lt Col Paul W.	017506	CE	Commandant

*wia 6th June 1944 Omaha Beach

Thompson WOJG Kendrick F. USA	Transportation Section	
Thorn 1st Lt Isaac. W.	Inf	Administration Officer, Amphibious
Tuttle 2nd Lt Richard P.	Inf	S-4 Section, Station Complement

Vaughan 1st Lt Earl D.   Chaplain, Special Staff

Warner Lt Col Morris T.	016562	Inf	

*promoted to Col and C O, School Troops

Watkins 1st Lt James M.	Inf	Administration Officer, Assault
Westerman Maj Harry K.	AGD	Adjutant, Special Staff
Wilkerson 2nd Lt Eugene L.	Inf	Attached, Infantry Section, Assault
Wolf Maj Edwin J.	CE	Chief, Assault Section, Amphibious

It must be noted that the majority of staff remained at the Assault Training Centre, although some junior posts were filled on rotation by officers from combat divisions. When the Centre began to wind down from March 1944 onwards, many officers requested postings to active combat units, or were simply re-assigned as their post was no longer relevant or required.

This list is not exhaustive and only shows personnel who are mentioned in official documents.

UNITS

1st FIGHTER GROUP USAAF

Sep 43   -   Participated in Hedge Hog exercise at Assault Training Centre with 175th Regimental Combat Team using 3 Medium bombers & 6 attack aircraft.

1st INFANTRY DIVISION "BIG RED ONE"

08 Feb 44	-	16th RCT took amphibious training to 26th Feb.
24 Feb 44	-	2nd Bn, 18th Inf Regt took amphibious training to 29th Feb.
15 Mar 44	-	3rd Bn, 18th Inf plus one platoon Cannon Company took amphibious training to 20th March.

4th INFANTRY DIVISION "IVY DIVISION"

25 Feb 44 - Movement Order #1. Hq 4th Infantry Div, APO 4, 25 Feb 1944.
"to participate in assault training for the period 1-15 Mar 1944,
at the United States Assault Training Center, Woolacombe, England."

UNIT	OFFICERS	WARRANT OFFICERS	ENLISTED MEN
8th Infantry Regiment			
(less 3d Bn & Bn Med Sec)	127	6	2525
Det, 12th Infantry Regiment	26	0	120
3d Bn & Bn Med Sec., 22d Inf	43	0	988
Det, 22nd Infantry Regiment	20	0	83
29th Field Artillery Battalion	36	2	570
Det, 42 Field Artillery Battalion	3	0	2
Det, 44 Field Artillery Battalion	3	0	2
Det, 20 Field Artillery Battalion	1	0	1
Co A, 4 Engineer Combat Battalion	7	0	194
Det, Co B, 4 Engineer Combat Bn	1	0	6
Co C, 4 Engineer Combat Bn	6	0	196
Det, 4 Signal Company	1	0	20
Det, 4 Medical Battalion	1	0	0
Co A, 4 Medical Battalion	6	0	112
Det, Co B, 4th Med Bn	3	0	3
Det, Co C, 4th Med Bn	3	0	3
Det, Adj Gen's Sec, Hq 4th Inf Div	1	0	4

11 Apr 44   - Movement Order #8. Cos A and C, 0237 Engineer Combat Battalion, report at the USATC, prior to 12 Apr 44, and upon completion of this temporary duty on or about 19 April 1944.

22 Apr 44   -   Movement Order #10. A detachment of the 4th Inf Div, and attached unit, consisting of the number of personnel from units as indicated below:

70 Tank Battalion	2 O	24 EM
Co A, 4 Engineer Combat Battalion	3	
Co B, ..	3	
Co C, ..	3	

Riley 1 Lt Benjamin J 01011260, Inf, 70th Tk Bn, is designated as detachment commander.

5th RANGER BATTALION

Mar 44   -   Arrived in UK, 34 Officers, 563 EM. To Scotland, Braunton, Devon, Swanage, Dorset for training.

May 44   -   "A group from the 2nd and 5th Ranger Battalions underwent a training period here of three and a half weeks, apparently slightly longer than was planned. Part of this was special purpose or rehearsal work. As the Assault Training Center is not involved in the higher levels of planning, it was necessary for the Rangers to tell us what they had to do and what was needed. All received the same individual training as the Regimental Combat Team 's but their team, company, and battalion exercises were modified as required. Like the Airborne troops, the Rangers were full of enthusiasm and were very proficient with their weapons. They were not as methodical and serious as some other units we have had and there was a tendency to horseplay. Their attitude resulted in improvising and opportunism, but this is fitting for the type of unit and they were alert and keen".

6th ENGINEER SPECIAL BRIGADE

May 44   -   " ... Thompson Colonel Paul W, the former Commanding Officer of the Center, conducted two exercises for groups of about 1,600 each. These consisted in landing, establishment of dumps, clearing beaches, construction of exits, etc. They did not involve any instruction by our staff, only the assignment of the areas and such incidental assistance as could be rendered. The units involved needed the opportunity for this sort of practice and the benefit should be correspondingly great. Their training in field sanitation and police had left much to be desired. The problems were well run and were favored by excellent weather."

8th FINANCE DISBURSING SECTION

03 Nov 43   -   At ATC with 2 Officers, 1 WO and 17 EM.

8th INFANTRY REGIMENT
4th Infantry Division

01 Mar 44   -   Regiment less 3rd Bn and Bn Med Sec - 127 Off, 6 WO, 2526 EM attended ATC for assault training.

16th INFANTRY REGIMENT
1st Infantry Division

08 Feb 44   -   16th RCT amphibious training at ATC until 26 Feb 44.

18th FIELD FORCE REPLACEMENT DEPOT

01 May 44   -   Assault Training Centre closed and handed over to this unit

18th INFANTRY REGIMENT
1st Infantry Division

24 Feb 44   -   2nd Bn to ATC for amphibious training until 29 Feb 44
15 Mar 44   -   3rd Bn plus one platoon Cannon Co to ATC for training

21st WEATHER SQUADRON

03 Nov 43   -   Det at ATC as part of Station Complement. Based at Woolacombe, Devon with 3 officers and 13 EM.

22nd INFANTRY REGIMENT
4th Infantry Division

01 Mar 44   -   3d Bn and Bn Med Sec of 43 Off, 988 EM attended ATC for amphibious training.
                  -     Detachment of 20 Off, 83 EM attended ATC for training.

28th INFANTRY DIVISION "Keystone"

27 Oct 43   -   Advance cadre at ATC

29th FIELD ARTILLERY BATTALION
4th Infantry Division

01 Mar 44   -   36 Off, 570 EM attended ATC for training until 15 Mar 44.

29th INFANTRY DIVISION

Dec 43   -   Completed training at ATC. Entire Division participated in concentration and processing for embarkation on Exercise Duck

38th CAVALRY RECONNAISSANCE SQUADRON

10 Feb 44   -   As part of 102nd Cavalry Group (Mecz), 2 tank platoons, 1 less tanks, and a troop of Hq attached to ATC until about 06 Mar 44.

24 Feb 44   -   Stone wall the property of The Stores, Croyde, Devon damaged by American army tank when proceeding from Georgeham, Devon to Croyde camp at approx 10 pm. Estimated damage £10. Tank driven by Denny Robert L TSgt 20743301, F Company, 38 Cav Recon Sqn.

27 Mar 44   -   Vehicular collision on bend opposite Mill Farm, Croyde, 4.55 pm between private m/car BUL 93 driven by Fl Off Leopold Antoniewicz, 304 Polish Squadron, Chivenor, Devon and a light US Army tank driven by Elrod Guy M T5 14126275, F Company, 38 Cavalry Recon Sqn, APO 230. Slight damage to car. Owner Sergeant B Janicki, 304 Sqn.

40th MOBILE COMMUNICATION SQUADRON

03 Nov 43   -   Det M at ATC as part of Station Complement. Based at Woolacombe, Devon with 8 EM.

42nd FIELD ARTILLERY BATTALION
4th Infantry Division

01 Mar 44   -   Det of 3 Officers and 3 EM attended ATC for amphibious training until 15 Mar 44.

44th FIELD ARTILLERY BATTALION
4th Infantry Division

01 Mar 44   -   Det 3 Off 2 EM attended ATC

70th TANK BATTALION

23 Apr 44   -   Attached to 0004 Infantry Division, attended ATC with 2 officers and 24 EM plus detachment of 4 Engineer Combat Battalion. Designated detachment commander Riley.

81st CHEMICAL BATTALION (MOTORIZED)

03 Nov 43	-	Company D at ATC as part of School Troops, based at Lincombe, Devon with 6 officers and 197 EM.
16 Mar 44	-	Ltr. Hq V Corps. Subject: Troop Movement. 16 March 1944. To: CO, 81st Chemical Bn (Mtz). "Co B, 81st Chemical Bn (Mtz) to be moved on or about 18 March 1944 for the purpose of participating in a period of combined training with 116th Regimental Combat Team, ending about 30 March 1944.
13 Apr 44	-	Ltr. Hq V Corps. Subject: Troop Movement, 13 Apr 1944. To: CO, 81st Cml Bn, Mtz. "1st Plat, Co B, 81st Cml Bn, Mtz. To be moved from present location to Croyde, Devon on 13 April 1944, and attached to Aslt Tng Cen. Upon completion of this training this platoon will return to home station.

101st AIRBORNE DIVISION "SCREAMING EAGLES"

Apr 44   -   Two groups of about 1000 men each attended ATC each received five days training in April. They were made up of composite units so that companies spread throughout the division would be trained. Again both the staff and the 101st felt it was valuable and regretted that more of them were not able to be in on it. Their assault training did not include dropping or landing by glider and of course no amphibious work. It assumed they had reached the area of their objective and started from that point. They did not use the 30 man assault team (based on the capacity of the LCVP), but proposed teams of parachute infantry platoons consisting of two officers and 35 men and glider infantry platoons of one officer and 46 men. A special area was turned over to them for their final assault problem and this was in the nature of a rehearsal. They showed exceptional energy and enthusiasm.

109th INFANTRY REGIMENT
28th Infantry Division

Nov 43   -   109th Regimental Combat Team trained at ATC

102nd CAVALRY GROUP (MECHANIZED)

04 Feb 44   -   Ltr. Hq V Corps. Subject: Troop movement. 4 Feb 1944. To: CO, 102nd Cavalry Group (Mecz) - to move on or about 10 February 1944. Two (2) Tank Platoons (1)(less tanks) and a Troop headquarters of the 0038 Cavalry Reconnaissance Squadron. One (1) 75mm Assault Gun Platoon with two (2) guns. To be attached until approximately 6 March 1944.

112th ENGINEER COMBAT BATTALION

17 Mar 44   -   Ltr Hq V Corps. Subject: Troop Movement. 17 Mar 1944. To: CO, 112th Engr (C) Bn. Co C, 112th Engr (C) Bn to be moved on 18 March 1944. This unit will be attached to 0116 Infantry Regiment for training only.

115th REGIMENTAL COMBAT TEAM
29th Infantry Division

05 Nov 43   -   Daily arrival and departure Reports, USATC, 5 Nov 1943.
115th RCT (29th Inf Div)
115th Infantry
110 Field Artillery Battalion
Co's A & C, 0121 Engineer Combat Battalion
Det A, MP Pln, 29th Inf
Det 29 Signal Company

116th INFANTRY REGIMENT
29th Infantry Division

01 Sep 43   -   Arrived at ATC for training
Mar 44   -   Refresher course at ATC

116th REGIMENTAL COMBAT TEAM

20 Mar 44   -   The 116th Regimental Combat Team returned for a refresher course during 20-29 Mar 44. This was the only unit to come back for a repetition of the Center's training and several interesting points were noted. They had kept in touch with our changes in technique and after thorough practice and numerous exercises engaged in during the winter, they felt that practically no variations were needed or desirable. The landing exercises were planned by them to be in the nature of rehearsals, and to that extent differed from previous instruction here. The weather permitted all to be made outside the estuary and the problems were very

good. Both the RCT and the staff here considered them entirely worthwhile. The improvement shown by the troops in those things they had done in October was obvious and encouraging. Though the organization was slightly modified there was no change in the 30 man boat team.

121st ENGINEER COMBAT BATTALION
29th Infantry Division

Sep 43   -   Assault Training Centre of training.

146th ENGINEER COMBAT BATTALION

17 Oct 43   -   Assigned to First U.S. Army, APO 230, upon arrival in Britain. To Lincombe Camp, Ilfracombe, North Devon.

27 Oct 43   -   Moved to the area of Saunton Sands beach to maintain an assault obstacle course.

05 Nov 43   -   Attached to U.S. Assault Training Center, Woolacombe, Devon, England until 4th April 1944. The Battalion's function at Braunton was the maintenance and erection of various courses and ranges for the United States Assault Training Center. This involved work at Woolacombe, Woolacombe Sands, Saunton Sands, Braunton Burrows, and Baggy Point. In connection with the work, allocation of heavy equipment to the Battalion was made necessary. The Battalion operated rock quarries and water points as well as helping to institute and maintain utilities service at Braunton Camp. The Battalion earned an enviable reputation for efficient work and members were commended on various occasions by Colonel Thompson, ATC CO.

04 Apr 44   -   Attached to 1121st Engineer Combat Group being deactivated about 01 Apr 44, the 146 ECB was attached shortly thereafter by Army Headquarters to V Corps and subsequently attached to the 1121 ECG at Newquay, Cornwall, England ... for training necessities.

13 Apr 44   -   Due to the exigencies of the situation, V Corps recalled the Battalion - first only Company A and then shortly after, the entire Battalion - to Braunton Camp and the former ATC training sites for intensive training for a specialised operation - the clearance of underwater and beach obstacles to aid the Allied assault upon the European mainland.

24 Apr 44   -   Company B and Company C arrived at Braunton. H & S Company arrived three days later.

14 May 44   -   Letter, Headquarters V Corps. Subject: Troop movement. To: Commanding Officer, 146th Engineer (C) Battalion.

Movement from ATC. 146th Engineer (C) Bn. Detachment,
127 vehicles and 236 enlisted men (build-up and residual
elements, from USATC to Newquay on or about 14 May
1944. Permanent change of station.

156th INFANTRY REGIMENT

Oct 43   -   Regiment, less Detachment attached to ATC as "School Troops"

03 Nov 43   -   Assault Training Centre - Woolacombe, Devon.

Unit	Location	Off	WO	EM
Hq Station Complement				
Hq Co, 156th Infantry (less)	Woolacombe	3	1	113
Service Co, 156th Infantry (less)	..	5	2	95
Det A, Co D, 156th Infantry	..	0	0	18
Det A, Med Det, 156th Infantry	..	2	0	21
Anti-Tank Co, 156th Infantry (less)	..	4	0	36
Co A, 156th Infantry	..	7	0	174
Hq & Hq Co, 3rd Bn, 156th Inf (less)	..		2	0
94				
Hq School Troops				
Det A, Hq, 156th Infantry	Ilfracombe	18	2	24
Co D, 156th Infantry (less)	Saunton Sands	6	0	149
Co L, 156th Infantry	..	6	0	102
Med Dept Det (less)	Ilfracombe	8	0	60
Hq & Hq Co, 2nd Bn, 156th Infantry	..	8	0	98
Det A, Hq Co, 3rd Bn, 156th Inf	..	1	0	33
Co E, 2nd Bn, 156th Infantry	..	6	0	188
Co F, 2nd Bn, 156th Infantry	..	6	0	186
Co G, 2nd Bn, 156th Infantry	..	6	0	190
Co H, 2nd Bn, 156th Infantry	..	5	0	160

Dec 43   -   FUSA Periodic Report, 11 Jan 44 for Dec 43. "156th Inf
Regt and 234 Engineer Combat Battalion atchd as school
troops conducted assault training for the following units:
Special troops, 29 Infantry Division
112 Engineer Combat Battalion
109 Regimental Combat Team
110 Regimental Combat Team
Officer cadre from 1 Infantry Division and 9 Infantry Division
Btry A, 771 Tank Destroyer Battalion
112 Regimental Combat Team
Co A, 0743 Tank Battalion
Co C & Co B, 0081 Chemical Battalion

07 Jan 44   -   Mr G.H.L. Frog Street Farm, Georgeham, Devon Farmer
reported that he was driving his small Austin m/van ETT

		288 towards Croyde, Devon about 9.45 am when approx 175 yards before reaching North Hole Farm, a US Army jeep coming from the opposite direction collided with the front offside of his van doing a considerable amount of damage. Driver of jeep gave LOVERING his name as Silvia T5 Melvin, L Coy, 156 Infantry, APO 553 US Army.
01 Mar 44	-	Vehicular collision 12.30 pm approx 175 yards Georgeham side of North Hole Farm between private m/car CRU 866 owned and driven by Dr J.A.R. of Braunton and US Army vehicle 20119415/s driven by Guidry Pvt Alvin J 20459369, Cannon Coy, 156 Infantry, APO 533.

162nd SIGNAL PHOTOGRAPHIC COMPANY

03 Nov 43	-	Assault Training Centre - Woolacombe, Devon. Det G as part of Hq Station Complement with 1 Officer and 6 EM.

197th QM GAS SUPPLY COMPANY

03 Nov 43	-	Part of ATC "Station Complement" with 2 officers and 72 EM located at Ilfracombe, Devon

197th REPLACEMENT COMPANY
50th Replacement Battalion

19 Jul 44	-	Report of Coastguard, Croyde, Devon that unknown female bather rescued from the sea at Croyde Bay in the afternoon by a coloured American soldier Johnson Pvt Rudolph 32910881 , 197 Replacement Company, Croyde Camp, and Garner T5 David A 15078994, A Company 771 Tank Destroyer Battalion, Saunton, Devon. Johnson before entering water handed his gold wrist watch to a female who was missing when he came out. Enquiries made and statement taken with a view to locating the female who held the watch, also the person who was rescued but with no result.
07 Aug 44	-	Mrs J.R.W. Shepherd Standing, Pinkney Green, Berkshire, temporary home at Home House, Croyde, age 44, married woman. Reports Kodak folding camera No A118 in brown leather case and two pairs of bathing trunks stolen from a locked beach hut on Croyde Burrows between 6.30 pm 6.8.44 and 11 am 7.8.44. US Army personnel suspected. Enquiries made by US Army CID agents. Camera found in possession of Pvt , 197 Replacement Company, APO 872 stationed at Croyde.

200th FIELD ARTILLERY BATTALION

Dec 43   -   FUSA Periodic Report for Dec 43. "received training at ATC.

203rd MP COMPANY

03 Nov 43   -   2 Traffic Platoon at ATC, based at Croyde, Devon with 1 officer and 55 enlisted men.

206th ENGINEERS

30 Apr 44   -   Report of A.B.T. Sub-Postmaster of Georgeham Post Office of damage to TK at Georgeham, Devon 10.15 pm by American service personnel. Leather holding straps torn from rivets on door and spring forced from fittings. Men responsible Sgt, A Company 206 Engineers, APO 230; Sfc, USN, Scouts and Raiders, US Navy.

234th ENGINEER COMBAT BATTALION

03 Nov 43   -   At ATC as component unit of "School Troops", based at Ilfracombe, Devon with 28 officers, 3 Warrant Officers and 627 enlisted men.

13 Dec 43   -   FUSA Periodic report for Nov 43. "Detail as school troops at the ATC allows no time for unit training"

256th SIGNAL CONSTRUCTION COMPANY

03 Nov 43   -   At ATC as part of "School Troops", based at Croyde, Devon with 1 officer and 30 enlisted men.

299th ENGINEER COMBAT BATTALION

14 May 44   -   Letter. Hq V Corps, Subject: Troop movement, 14 May 1944. To: CO, 299th Engineer (C) Bn. "299th Engineer (C) Battalion Detachment, 237 enlisted men (build-up and residual elements) from USATC to Paneswick Manor Camp on or about 14 May 1944.

313th FIELD HOSPITAL

31 Jul 44   -   Body of 2 Lt J.B. attached to 45 Replacement Battalion US Army, Braunton, Devon found on Saunton Sands approx 8.30 am. Deceased had been bathing at Saunton Sands on 30 Jul 44 with other officers but had not been reported as

missing. Body identified by 2nd Lt Alexander E Woodside of same unit. Body removed to Braunton mortuary and later to 313 American Field Station Hospital at Fremington, Devon. Buried at Cambridge American Cemetery.

363rd QM SERVICE COMPANY

03 Nov 43   -   At ATC as part of Hq Station Complement, based at Ilfracombe, Devon with 48 EM.

398th ENGINEER GENERAL SERVICE REGIMENT

Aug 43   -   Companies C and E were located one and two miles, respectively, west of Braunton. Company D established itself one mile north of Bideford. Company F set up camp a half mile south of Croyde. And Second Battalion Headquarters operated from Saunton Sands.

453rd AMPHIBIOUS TRUCK COMPANY

03 Nov 43   -   At ATC as part of "School Troops", based at Croyde, Devon with 7 officers and 175 EM.

07 Dec 43   -   21 personnel, 57 vehicles assigned to 5 Engineer Special Brigade under 131 QM Mobile Battalion.

460th ANTI AIRCRAFT ARTILLERY AUTOMATIC WEAPONS BATTALION

28 Mar 44   -   Ltr. Hq V Corps. Subject: Troop movement. To: CO, 460th AAA AW Bn. "To be moved on 29 Mar 1944 for training".

507th MP BATTALION

13 Apr 44   -   Ltr. Hq V Corps. Subject: Troop Movement. 13 Apr 1944. To: CO, Co A, 507th MP Bn. "Movement from ATC. 1st Pln, Co A, 507th MP Bn. To be moved from Woolacombe, Devon to Norton Manor Camp by 22 Apr 1944. This detachment is relieved from temporary duty with U.S. Assault Training Center effective 210001B, April 1944. Permanent change of station.

509th MP BATTALION

03 Nov 43   -   3 Platoon, Company C at ATC as part of Station Complement, based at Woolacombe, Devon with 1 officer and 57 EM

553rd ARMY POSTAL UNIT

03 Nov 43   -   At ATC as part of Station Complement, based at Woolacombe, Devon with 1 officer and 11 EM

634th ANTI AIRCRAFT (AUTOMATIC WEAPONS) BATTALION

03 Nov 43   -   Battery "D" at ATC as part of School Troops

745th TANK BATTALION

03 Nov 43   -   At ATC as part of School Troops, based at Croyde, Devon with 5 officers and 141 EM

802nd SIGNAL SERVICE BATTALION

03 Nov 43   -   Detachment at ATC as part of Station Complement, based at Woolacombe, Devon with 2 EM

810th SIGNAL SERVICE BATTALION

03 Nov 43   -   Detachment at ATC as part of Station Complement, based at Woolacombe, Devon with 4 EM

3409th ORDNANCE MEDIUM AUTOMOTIVE MAINTENANCE COMPANY

03 Nov 43   -   At ATC Woolacombe, Devon with 4 officers and 116 EM

3422nd ORDNANCE MEDIUM AUTOMOTIVE MAINTENANCE COMPANY

03 Nov 43   -   ATC Station Complement at Ilfracombe, Devon with 4 officers and 116 EM